THE HAPPY VOYEUR:

A Psychological Study

by

Wilson H. Guertin, PhD

Follow the author, an experienced Clinical Psychologist, as he takes you into the scheming mind of voyeur, Abraham Murray. Dr. Guertin employs a fictional stalker for the main character in this narrative to re-create typical case material for you to ponder. His efforts are proceeded by "Fifty Shades of Grey," and "Memoirs of a Geisha," both of which try to present live pictures of deviant persons.

By following this unforgettable journey you may acquire some of the skills required to understand a man obsessed with sex. For the first time you have the opportunity to make some sense out of a world that everybody else dismisses as "crazy." Read and learn about an exciting and dangerous life. Get to know a so-called "sex maniac."

This book is anything but a child's story-- it is loaded with sexual matter. The framework of this creation is Freudian and as such, there is a strong emphasis on psychosexual development. Also, you must consider the institutional setting where diversions are limited and sex is readily available

The book is for mature readers only.

THE HAPPY VOYEUR:

A Psychological Study

by

Wilson H. Guertin, PhD

ALSO BY JONATHAN P. SLOW

BIBLICAL FIGURES:
I, Joseph, Father of Jesus. **2012. Amazon**
I, Mary, Mother of Jesus. **2013. Amazon**

THE SEXIEST DETECTIVE:
The Sexiest Detective in West Florida. **2013, Amazon**
The Sexiest Detective in Key West. **2013, Amazon**
The Sexiest Detective in Ireland. **2013, Amazon**

PSYCHOLOGICAL ANALYSIS:
A Desirable Killing and the Paranoid Mind. **2013, Amazon**
The Shrink, Who Stole my Life. **2014, Amazon**

CROSS-CULTURAL:
Beware the Beneficent Gringo! **2013, Amazon**
Martin Provost, Survivor. **2015, Amazon**

ADVENTURE / SPY STORIES:
Istanbul's Silent Witness. **2014, Amazon**
Istanbul's Secret Warriors. **2014, Amazon**
Jonathan Padraig Slow, **Exposed. 2014, Amazon**
Pirates and Oriental Slave Trading. **2015, Amazon**
The Making of an American Jihadist, 2015, Amazon

THE HAPPY VOYEUR

by

WILSON H. GUERTIN, PhD

Copyright © 2016

This book is covered by international copyright and thereby protected from being reproduced or transmitted in any form or by any means, electronic or mechanical, including writing, photocopying, recording, taping, or by any information storage and retrieval system or in any other manner used illegally....

This is a work of fiction. Names, characters, places, and incidents are the products of the author's imagination or are used fictitiously. Any resemblance to actual events, locales, or persons, living or dead, is entirely coincidental.

Cover picture by Shutterstock.com

Cover by Bear

First Edition

Ж

BEST

PYCHOLOGICAL NOVEL

The

FLORIDA MYSTERY WRITERS

2015

"**Voyeurism** is the sexual interest in or practice of spying on people engaged in intimate behaviors, such as undressing, sexual activity, or other actions usually considered to be of a private nature."

Hirschfeld, M. 1938

Prevalence

"...Forty-two percent of college males, who had never been convicted of a crime had watched others in sexual situations."

Wikipedia.

THE SHIT STORM

Narrated by Abraham Murray

HAPPY VOYEUR

NEWPORT, RI

The whisper of steel on steel grated on my nerves. Jails aren't designed to make prisoners feel comfortable. But the public sleeps better knowing that a dangerous sex offender had been captured.

I startled a little as the lockbolts snapped into place to announce that I was stored away safely-- once again, the beast was caged. The city was quiet and its citizens sighed with relief because they knew that there would be one less maniac skulking around their homes that night.

I was a respectable 22-year-old student of Anthropology at Boston University, although I may not have seemed like it. It would be more accurate to say that I *was* a respectable citizen until I got caught peeking in the windows of an apartment with the evidence of the crime in my hand.

The admission statement showed that I was apprehended while trespassing on private property at night and engaging in lewd behavior. The arresting officer declared that I resisted arrest when the private security guard apprehended me. It alleged that I attempted to escape by assaulting the uniformed guard. The report claimed that I had to be subdued by the police officer so that I could be transported to the booking station.

I normally display self-confidence, but I was intimidated by the whole process of being arrested and booked. The system was designed to force submission and assure compliance. I was not used to being ordered around and the officers knew it.

The police branded me as their prisoner as they wrestled me down to the ground at the apartment complex. I wore their ignominious handcuffs until we got back to the police station. The cops pushed and shoved me to enhance my subordination. They were reminding me that I was nothing more than a piece of shit.

They were just polite enough to avoid charges of showing gross disrespect for a citizen in their care. There were other little things about the way I was handled that irked me. One officer gave me the respect all citizens are due-- he addressed me as *Mr*. Murray. However, the others felt the need to teach me to keep my place and remain compliant. They just called me by my last name.

Police always use these softening-up techniques to make their job easier with detainees. What else could I expect under those circumstances? If my skin were darker, they would have called me just "Boy."

When they walked me to the next station in the booking process, they grasped me roughly by the arm and dragged me along. They seemed to enjoy reminding me that they were the masters of the city.

* * * * *

Our family name is Murray and I am Abraham. We used to be proud of the family name. It was a good old name from the days of the British Ascendency in Ireland. We always insisted that the family name of Murray was Norman-British. My ancestor had moved from Britain to Ireland to manage a large estate that Oliver Cromwell granted him for service to his faction.

My Great-great-grandfather left Ireland to come over to settle in Rhode Island 200 years ago. Communal effort converted primitive Rhode Island wilderness into one of the nicest places to live in America. The Newport beaches and harbor were admired by all, but only the rich could afford to build there.

We always took pains to exclude the working class, immigrant types from diminishing our restricted neighborhood. Building permits were issued only to those with pale skins and either Norman or Anglo-Saxon names. Even the Irish were unwelcome unless they had money like my family had.

Our family home in Newport was one of the first mansions to burst forth from the virgin soil. It was constructed on 100 acres of scrub forest that isolated us from annoying intrusions. The house of 20 rooms gave each resident further isolation, even from other family members. We were a dynasty sufficient unto ourselves.

* * * * *

Great-grandfather came to New York when he was still a boy, but he had the heart of a man. Each day he went out alone into the bay in his little boat and returned with his catch. He sold his fish at the docks without depending upon any middleman fishmongers. He worked day and night so that he could buy a larger boat. He continued to sell his catch in the same location until he accumulated enough savings to purchase an even larger sail-equipped fishing-boat.

Within ten years Great-grandfather had a small fleet of fishing boats and the crews to work them. Over the subsequent ten years he converted his fleet from fishing boats into profitable cargo-transporting ships. By the time he retired, he had completed all the additions to our Newport mansion and he was the owner of a profitable maritime shipping firm.

Great-grandfather always used to say that his success was due to marrying well, working hard, and honoring his Irish ancestors-- the Leprechauns. It certainly was true that he married well-- his father-in-law was a rich merchant. That was the only way he would have been able to acquire investment capital fast enough to match his ambitions.

Great-grandfather's wife's father inherited a very profitable trading enterprise and had a bigger cash flow than he knew what to do with.

Later, my Grandfather came to depend upon his father to put much of that capital to work to expand their shipping fleet. By the time the rich father-in-law died, most of the business was owned jointly by my grandfather and my father.

Over the years they built more docks, and they expanded the original shipyard. Grandfather was clever enough to eliminate competition by purchasing several smaller shipping companies. The days of struggle were over and Grandfather turned over most of the business to be managed by his assistants so that he could enjoy the comforts of our mansion in Newport.

But everything changes. The secluded, peaceful life at Newport could not last. Within a few decades the rich New Yorkers started seeking refuge from their crowded city. Not only the landscape changed, so did the people. The old pioneer-spirited settlers were replaced by self-indulgent youths.

We always were important people. The decline began with my grandfather, who was a gambler and an alcoholic. From time to time he would try to restore our good name and fortune, but ended up conducting us along the path of corruption and dissipation. People clawed at Grandfather, as if they were bringing down a wounded animal in the hunt.

The earlier generations bore our name proudly, but later it was subjected to ridicule. Rich New Yorkers were becoming a nuisance. The immigrants coming to America from Ireland even denied that our name was

Irish. The public whispered around that we were really immigrant Jews from London's Whitechapel district.

Other members of Newport society were proud of their family heritages. Their coats of arms carried reminders of how they were rewarded by the Crown for their brave support in battle. The envious newcomers denied us the same right to honor our ancestors. They joked that our family had gained title to our estates by trickery, rather than by brave service.

You can't dispel demeaning gossip, because it is based in intangible hatred rather than on information. I ignored those rumors. There was little else I could do with a first name like Abraham. "How could my father have agreed to name me that! Why couldn't he have named me Sean or Michael?

The Murray empire was pulled down by competitors as well as by bad management. Ultimately, the shipping corporation's debts outweighed company assets. Bankruptcy couldn't be postponed any longer and the corporation was dissolved.

Each of us managed to walk away with a few hundred thousand dollars, but we still felt poor. We no longer received a large director's annual salary for sitting in board meetings once a month. If we wanted more income we had to go out and earn it.

Father gave up the mansion in Newport when he retired. It was part of the corporate holdings and Father did nothing to preserve it from being sold along with the bankrupt business. The collapse of our empire came just prior to WWI. If Father had held off bankruptcy for one more year, the need to transport war materiel would have doubled our assets in just four years. The new owners made a fortune overnight from wartime shipping. We were left with the, "Packing papers it came in."

* * * * *

My parents purchased a six-bedroom house that was comfortable, but it lacked the luxuries of the old one. No live-in servants attended us to make it possible to give lavish weekend parties for ten or more guests. I was a slimmed-down version of my ancestors of old.

I lived there with the parents for a few years. It was a big comedown from starting out life in a 20-room house with half a dozen house servants.

Here I was sitting in my tiny cell, dejected about my status. I regretted that I had not been more careful to retain the community's respect. In short, I had let everyone down, including myself. Don't misunderstand me and think that I regretted pursuing perverted sexual pleasures. No, I was just suffering the remorse of a criminal, who was caught at the scene of his crime.

As I sat idly on my bunk, I recalled the early days when nobody would have dared to arrest a member of our Newport family. Now they could throw me into jail without hesitation. The early capital of goodwill toward the family had been dissipated over the past decades by ungrateful offspring. Even all my efforts to live a commendable life were nullified by getting caught like a common criminal

As I sat on my bunk I reflected on the way people would view me now that my secret indulgences were coming to light. Some would pretend to be sorry for me. "Pity is a luxury that the rich can afford." The vultures would hop all over my carcass looking for the chance to avenge themselves. They envied the rich and blamed them for everything.

* * * * *

My whole life was built around an image of social respectability. Now I had to perpetuate the appearance of being a quiet, conscientious citizen faced with the consequences of careless misbehavior. I had to be a repentant child, who was the victim of temptation.

This picture of respectability would be an essential cover throughout my life of skirting the law. I needed to appear ordinary while secretly pursuing my voyeuristic impulses. I didn't want to fight the law; there always were so many of them against poor little me.

My attorney, Horace B. Digbee, was the perfect member of the community to help me salvage my life. He was a Newport gentleman, who reeked of respectability. He was the only partner of his commercial law office, who deigned to handle a criminal case as an accommodation for special business clients.

Mr. Digbee entered the portal of the courthouse as if he owned the building and expected the scattered workers to come over and kiss his hand. He was a marvel at role-playing. He projected importance without being arrogant enough to ruffle other people's feathers. In short, he was in command, and at the same time he exuded a friendly gentleness. Role-playing was his profession, so God only knows what he really was like inside. Mr. Digbee was not the sort of man that the police would ask to sit in a waiting room while someone fetched me.

He uttered an ambiguous "Harrumph" as they took him right to my cell and opened the door apologetically. The police allowed him to take the initiative. He had me conducted to an office where we wouldn't be surrounded by the depressing ambience of a holding cell.

I had spent lots of time thinking about how to exist comfortably in a society laced with traps to catch sex offenders. I could have told Mr. Digbee how to direct our efforts in my case, but I thought it best to let him reach his own conclusions. He expected to earn his considerable fee.

He soon came to agree with my analysis. We should not waste time on building a useless defence. Instead, we would focus on seeking that rare commodity-- pity for the unfortunate sex offender. We wanted the judge to see me as the victim of a sudden, uncontrollable impulse. I was to appear so remorseful that even the angels would cry.

We had to develop a scenario that contrasted my temporary misbehavior with my customary law-abiding life as a model citizen. It was fairly easy to obtain a succession of character witnesses, and I was quite ready to display my profound remorse. We still needed to find some external provocation that led me to such atypical behavior.

We would play the, "I wasn't my real self" card. We would make it easy for the sentencing judge to discover that I had been drinking at a bar on the night in question. "Yes, Your Honor, I know that alcohol has a strong effect on me, so I generally avoid it."

I had a brush with the police once before. Mr. Digbee was aware of my past record, but he hoped that it would not come up in court. We hoped to get by with six-month's probation. That would have been too easy! The prosecution used this past record, as a reason for the judge to bring jail-time back on the table.

We couldn't have the judge coming to view me as a repetitive sex offender, who never pays for his crimes. If he did, he would have to send me to prison. As a common criminal I would face a long prison term. However, if we tried to evade the criminal route, I would end up being tagged with the sexual offender label.

The discussion in-chambers with the presiding judge revealed that he could be expected to hand down a five-year criminal sentence if we persisted in entering a not guilty verdict.

A $50,000 retainer brought the noted criminal lawyer Allyn Dershowits into the affray. He announced publically that he would be presenting my defence to a jury. The judge didn't want to turn his courtroom into a circus, so he backed down a little.

Informal discussion revealed that I had two choices-- to spend five years in prison as a convict, or be remanded to a mental health treatment facility. A further condition for hospitalization was that I could not be released during the first six months. Furthermore, they could held me involuntarily for an additional year if I wasn't considered safe to release back into society.

If I chose the hospitalization, it would be as a "sexual psychopath." With either court order I would remain under monthly supervision during the first year following my release. Whether I would be placed into the parole system or receive outpatient follow-up depended upon the circumstances.

I decided to wear the stigma of being a known sexual offender rather than be sentenced to do hard time in prison. Mr. Digbee made a lot of trips to work out a deal with an Assistant D.A. Mr. Dershowits went back to New York with his fat retainer fee. It took several weeks to assemble the necessary affidavits as to character, along with a copy of my guilty plea and a formal petition for leniency in sentencing.

I took the risk of going for the shorter term even though it would create the opprobrium of being on the Sex Offender list. I decided to use my personal assets to carry me through to an early conclusion of all these constraints that were being placed upon my life. I still had enough self-confidence to carry it off. People liked me when they met me; I looked respectable and had a pleasant demeanor.

You probably think that I was concerned about being locked away from my family, like a wild animal. You probably believe that I wanted to be released in the shortest possible time so that I could live a normal life. Not so! I only wanted to have the constraints on me removed as soon as possible so I could go back to obtaining gratification from my voyeuristic games.

Hospitalization would give me at least half a year to sit around planning how to avoid getting caught again in such compromising situations. There even would be sufficient time to elaborate strategies to bring me greater satisfaction. I might get lucky enough to make friends with other voyeur patients and pick up a few pointers from them. If there were enough of us we could start a club for voyeurs!

* * * * *

As I stood before the judge, I looked like a businessman at a corporate board meeting. I appeared dejected and ashamed, but my amiable acceptance of my misfortune came through. There was no danger that the judge would mistake me for one of the hostile riffraff that he usually dealt with.

As I stood before him, he looked me over and the corners of his mouth rose slightly, as he involuntarily bent this head slightly toward me. It would be inappropriate for him to bestow his personal approval on a common criminal. Nonetheless, I could see that he was suppressing a smile. I hadn't lost all my charm. I was reassured that I could use it to advantage at the treatment facility.

The judge accepted my guilty plea and asked for presentencing testimony. He sighed with relief when he was assured that the court would not be bogged down listening to an endless string of character witnesses. Mr. Digbee just smiled at the judge and requested permission to submit affidavits attesting to the good character of his client. Everybody was happy to dispose of this case and get on with life

The judge leafed through the exhibits and announced that he already had seen most of them and felt confident that he could return a sentence after spending an hour or so in chambers. We broke for lunch and then returned for sentencing that afternoon at 3:00 o'clock. He prefaced the sentencing with a brief summary of his understanding of the case before him:

"The court takes note of the following:

A. The defendant has been a respected member of our community in the past.

B. In a weak moment, defendant acted on impulse and broke the law.

C. No other citizen was damaged materially by defendant's misbehavior.

D. Defendant has admitted fault in failing to exercise control over his behavior.

E. Defendant shows remorse and asks that he be given treatment to help him deal with his problem.

In view of the above, it is the opinion of this court that the defendant's illegal action should be viewed as a personal behavior problem rather than as an ordinary crime.

Therefore, the defendant is to be placed in a facility offering him residential treatment until he is judged ready for discharge. In no case shall he be restored into society until he completes a period of six-month residence. After his release from the facility, his adaptation to the community will be reviewed monthly by a qualified psychologist, parole officer, or social worker. A year after supervised follow-up he will be eligible for unconditional release from further court supervision."

At the conclusion of the session, the judge beckoned to Mr. Digbee for us to approach the bench. He looked down at me with all the Wisdom of Solomon and said, "Son, you are too smart to be here in my court. Courts are society's last resort to control its citizens. In the future keep your fly zipped or avoid apartment complexes that are well patrolled."

The judge sent me up for six months. I wasn't repentant, just sorry that I got caught and sent away. This action scored my record permanently as a sex-offender. At last I made the honor roll!

The gavel sounded and the judge departed. The rest of the crowd went home to enjoy a home-cooked meal with family. I tightened my belt bravely and walked away proudly to the new destiny that had been imposed upon me

* * * * *

I knew that the family was broken-hearted because of the disgrace I brought them. They were disappointed because incarceration would prevent me from completing my doctoral studies. I shamed the family name and realized that I should leave Rhode Island to go somewhere that my background was unknown.

FAMILY HISTORY

Narrated by Abraham Murray

MOTHER

If you are reading this recounting of my secret life, then I probably am dead. I was, a respected member of the community, so I would hate to disillusion my acquaintances with my innermost secrets. I hope you will respect my last wishes and not make them public knowledge.

The readers of the morning newspaper are fascinated by accounts of the crimes of sexual perverts. It has not been easy to keep my name from appearing in those salacious accounts. I'm glad that few ever got to read about my sexual peccadilloes. Only my carefully recruited confederates have knowledge of my sexual activities, and even they have no idea what really goes on in my head. People see me as I want them to see me, and not as I really am.

If you are reading this account it's probably because you are interested in the life of a voyeur. You wonder what it's like to be a weirdo, so you won't be very interested in my food preferences for breakfast. You will want to learn about my naughty needs-- what turned me on. I did have things on my mind other than sex, but you probably can't be bothered to hear about them. Anyhow, nothing could be more intriguing than the revelations of a sex maniac.

* * * * *

All of us wonder about ourselves-- what made me like I am? God feels that He should be given all the credit for what we are. The Freudians want to blame it all on mothers. It's only fair to give mothers their due since they had to put up with squalling, stinking messes for the first couple of years.

Ask the preacher why I'm like I am. He knows: "He's got the Devil in him. If he went to church regularly, he would have a clean soul, not one engulfed with sexual ideas and impulses."

The chief of police knows where I took the wrong turn: "The police should have locked him up and thrown away the key when the patrol found him wandering around at night in an apartment complex."

My teacher blames herself for not making me study harder. Even my father wants to take some of the blame: "I should have beaten the shit out of him more often."

Probably Dad was right. The "No!" pronounced by a loving parent brings utter disappointment to a sensitive child. That act will go automatically into his cognitive storehouse as "Sin." In the future, that child will try to avoid actions that evoke disapproval.

As for myself, I am pretty well satisfied with the life I've lived. I managed to get a good education and to become a respected professor in my field. I have avoided jail cells for the most part, even though I was "hauled in" once or twice. Despite my strange ways of enjoying life, I maintained enough semblance to being normal to stay connected to the community.

I never had friends, only confederates. My special ways of enjoying life were too weird to share with others. On the positive side, this lessening of personal contact with others relieved me from the necessity for being sociable. I was able to concentrate on gratifying my selfish pleasures.

Like other children, I grew up being shaped by the family. It was my good fortune to have an older brother and sister precede me. They inured Mother to the disagreeable trials of infancy. She spent her youth in the drudgery of housekeeping and mothering my two siblings.

When she brought me home from the hospital, she advised father that no longer would she be the only servant for the entire family. She insisted that he employ a nanny and a housekeeper. That freed her up to live the last of her fleeting youth as a self-indulgent, charmer.

She used her allure to attract admiration from all the males she encountered. Conversely, she won the distain and enmity of all their wives. Mother kept quite busy playing the vamp and had little time to regret not having genuine friends. She used to put on airs even within the family. She felt safest letting her guard down with me because I was the youngest and most loving. We started out being intimate friends and remained such until her early demise.

Mother was my first and best confederate in this game of life. She needed me because she knew I needed her. We were both socially deprived people, who led normal-appearing lives, but only because we hid our thoughts and impulses from nosy strangers.

Ours was a necessary bond, a healthy one. It developed when she first took me to her breast. I was but a baby and so I couldn't be accused of stealing her affection from the rest of the family, but she was all mine from the start. She smothered me with affection, and I loved it.

At the same time you could see the wall of resentment going up between the rest of the family and me. During my first year we spent most of the time in her bedroom, with me clasped to the breast. She seldom invited my brother or sister into her quarters, but condescended to fuss over them a little at mealtime. The woman hired as a nanny spent her time looking after my older brother and sister. She babysat me only when mother wanted to take a nap.

When mother was tired of playing dress-ups, we would cuddle together in the big bed. With your dirty mind, you probably will be expecting me to tell you about how she taught me to want some sort of perverted satisfaction from future companions. Sorry to disappoint you but my seduction and training were quite subtle and proper. Nonetheless, that determined my whole future.

I developed a fetish for two things that I can trace back to those early experiences. Mother usually wore rubber gloves when changing my shitty diaper. She would reach out her gloved hands and pick me up to give me a hug and a kiss. Then she would wash my bottom with warm water and suds. It felt good and my unconscious stored away that pleasant learned sequence that incorporated the feel of the gloves.

The other residual from those days was the predilection for wearing girl's panties. I vaguely recall Mother wrapping up my face in her warm panties when she removed them from the clothes drier. She may have teased me with her naughty ideas, but I couldn't be expected to remember that part.

Perhaps it wasn't her warm panties that she wrapped me in-- maybe it was towels or something like that. The trouble with childhood recollections is that we fabricate and reconstruct them to fit our adult needs. The process of distortion is a protection from recognizing hidden desires in ourselves. This defensive process is called "retrospective falsification," better known as "wishful thinking."

* * * * *

Mother taught me to be a book lover. As such, I became a passive observer of other people's impulses and secrets. My earliest passion involved sneaking off to my room to read about the lives and exploits of others. I learned to enjoy being a witness to other people's activities. Mother wanted to do everything for me and she wouldn't let me take risks. I was just a child and a pampered one at that.

She never left me alone in the bathtub until I started school. Is it normal for a mother to bathe her five-year-old son? I honestly don't know. I just liked having her with me all the time. Maybe that's why I think she bathed me until I was five-years-old. Perhaps this too is an example of retrospective falsification. It seems more likely that she let me bath alone by the time I was two.

I was totally dominated by Mother and I basked in her light. She never let me encounter unfamiliar situations, so I didn't get to make decisions. Of course, Mother chose the books we read together. Somehow, she must have realized that she was preventing me from doing exciting things on my own. Later, she provided me with action stories when I was old enough to express my preferences.

Some of my favorite stories were those by Rudyard Kipling. I was able to experience the excitement of real men, living their lives bravely. Stories about pirates were also my favorites. I still remember how I pretended that I was the captain of the ship, who held absolute power over the ladies.

I was able to share the excitement of other's lives by reading-- I didn't need much more. I had a mother, who adored me, and I was presented with a world of action, even though it only consisted of words in a book.

I didn't spend all my time just pouring over the written word. I learned that searching for illustrations could be rewarding. All naughty little boys wear out the covers of the National Geographic magazines. Bare-breasted African princesses with tits of angels are hidden in each volume. Maybe my voyeuristic adventures were abetted by some forgotten African safari.

Reading in itself is innocuous, but my adolescent passion crept along into the channel of vulgar voyeurism. I memorized the pictures of ladies in the underwear section of Sears catalog, and it became my bible. I became the judge of a beauty contest as I lined the girls up in my mind.

Maybe I would have been more normal sexually if Mother hadn't nurtured my obsession with books. Without her encouragement I wouldn't have learned to appreciate the visual gratification that is so important in my life.

Very early on, I learned that I had no reason to envy others and their possessions. None had such a loving and attentive mother as mine. I was not wanting in any material way, either. I was never constrained by physical circumstances, only by the limits of my imagination.

Mother encouraged me to enter a fairy world of the para-natural. I didn't need toys like metal trucks and tin soldiers. I populated my living space with thoughts, ideas, and wishes. If I craved a temporary companion, I would conjure up an "Imaginary Playmate."

My worldly life was rich but my private world was even more gratifying. I lacked for nothing. I was suspended in a period of blissful time and had no wish to grow up and move on. I am still that child in many ways.

I was growing up like the runt of our litter, at least that's the way outsiders viewed me. Teachers and Mother's friends wanted to attach labels to me. I was in serious danger of falling into the hands of the professionals, who wanted to stick me with the label-Attention Deficit Disorder. The label would have followed me all my life if I were so identified.

Professionals are so silly! Sometimes I didn't respond when they spoke to me, because I would be focused on something else other than them. They had no common sense. When I was too absorbed in my own thoughts to answer them, they wanted to slap the ADD label on me.

Fortunately, Mother understood and would have none of it. I was her little boy and always would remain so. She was a gentle soul, so I tried to adopt her benign, non-confrontational manner of dealing with the world.

I identified with the wolf boy Mowgli, and I shared the excitement of his life. When Gunga Din the water bearer was in trouble so was I. As I grew a little older I was able to cut myself off almost completely from the rest of the world. I would sit for hours reading by myself, enjoying the worldly gratifications described in the books. I learned to channel my expectations for gratification into those printed words that could transport me into other worlds outside myself.

I was self-centered and unsocial, and yet I learned to love this world of self-gratification that could be pursued passively by reading books. I was relieved from exerting myself excessively and still was permitted to experience an exciting world. You can use your brains to circumvent effort if you are bright like me. People always said about me, "He got by in life with his brains."

As I grew older I kept expanding the horizons of my world. At that point, one of my favorite books was Gulliver's Travels, the political satire by the Irishman, Jonathan Swift. I would be transported to the mysterious lands as I picked up the volume to continue where I left off. Perhaps, "Transported" is not the best word to describe my changed condition; "transformed" better denotes my deeply altered state. I actually lived Gulliver's adventures when I shared his exploits.

So you can see how a mysterious cocoon was woven around me that limited my contact with a material world. I was retreating from reality but at the same time, I was allowed to enter the fictional world with its own kind of reality. There are two great things about the fictional world: You can dump it if it becomes threatening or boring, and the other is that you can modify it easily to suit your wishes.

You will say, "It sounds like you had a pleasant childhood, but it didn't prepare you to go out and meet the real world." You would be right. But you would be overlooking one thing-- it is quite possible to live a passive life if someone will provide you the support you need. Just observe any withdrawn schizophrenic on a hospital ward. He lives quite successfully without having to face the challenges of an outside world.

You may be wondering if I was headed for the passive, constricted life of one of those schizophrenics. I wondered about that too in late adolescence and early adulthood. I outgrew those concerns for the future as I grew older and developed more self-confidence.

My self-conscious concerns about the type of a life I would live diminished with my successes. I was a very contented person, who was fairly comfortable with others. I liked myself and enjoyed my life-style. Other people only knew as much as I wanted them to know about me, so they were friendly and companionable. I kept my secret dream-life to myself.

FATHER

My father was born in Newport mansion and lived there all his life. I grew up in our smaller 10-room house in the elite part of Newport. I brought home a new wife, and continued to live there with her and our daughter, until our divorce.

I was closer to my parents before my marriage. My wife never did hit it off with my mother, so each of our two families stayed in different parts of the house. We joined the parents for dinner every Sunday to make nice and to get caught up on the news.

Father was sociable but not very friendly. Do you understand the difference? He used to disappear on social binges, accompanied by his friends. I remember being jealous of their relationship with my father, because he should belong to me.

He continued to remain respectable and to maintain the Murray standing in the community, as best he could. He brought in enough income from the family business to maintain us, and still pay for drinking and gambling splurges. I wish Father had spent more time with Mother and me.

My father didn't employ a lot of set rules. His treatment of me was based upon, the circumstances of the time. He wasn't overly strict-- he let me learn to set my own limits. He disciplined me through showing his approval or disapproval. Most important, he taught me not to reveal myself to others.

Members of a family develop persistent attitudes toward one another according to their experience with each other. Father was a flexibly interactive sort of man. Perhaps I emulated him in my loose acceptance of legal constraints.

* * * * *

Family life is similar for all of us; only the details differ. After the courtship period, a wife is expected to adapt to the husband in marriage. She builds new expectancies and behavior to help her adapt successfully to the new life. Similarly, the husband changes his attitudes and expectances, too. The introduction of a newborn addition to the family creates the need for everyone to adapt to the new circumstances. Some adapt and others divorce or leave home. Family living proceeds on a rocky road!

The patterns of sibling interaction become fixed over time. Young children struggle in competition with each other because parents usually offer insufficient love to allow for sharing. Hostile behavior of siblings and the attitudes behind it are conveniently gathered under the Sibling Rivalry rubric.

Eventually a hierarchy will be formed and one child will come out as the favorite, and the others will be ordinary. Life is unfair but that's the way it is. Parents usually struggle to hide the favoritism, but the snake that destroys families from within will creep out inevitably.

I longed for a companionable father-son relationship but never really had one. Father was more than 40 years old when I was born. He was too grown up to play with babies. When I grew older, my own interests were too active or too childish for him to participate in. He was in the background as an authority figure, but he also tried to assure me that I could go to him in need or in trouble.

When I was 16, Father invited me to accompany him to New York City on a business trip. It turned out that that our time together was really a surprise birthday gift.

We stayed in a nice hotel, the one the family always used. Grandfather was the one, who started going there more than half a century earlier. Now, after so many years, the hotel had lost its glimmer and the neighborhood was filling up with new immigrants. These changes didn't discourage father from lodging there because he rather liked the more lively ways of the lower classes.

The hotel restaurant was still first class. Father even knew some of the diners making a night of it. Our family was known even outside Newport, although we were no longer influential.

Eating well was no novelty, so I enjoyed having new experiences in dining. We went to German, Italian , Greek, and French restaurants. The English I heard spoken was pronounced with many differing accents. I was surrounded by these different atmospheres, and had a chance to familiarize myself with interesting foreign dishes.

Perhaps it was that very special week I spent with Father that influenced me most in my choice of an academic specialty. I had never heard the word anthropology, but I found the mankind in New York interesting. It was like going on a cultural field trip.

I met some women on that trip, too. In fact, I encountered one woman there, who interested me more than any of the men.

We went out after dinner and walked a few blocks down the street. I asked Father where we were going. He grinned at me and said, "I'll take you to a very naughty place if you promise not to tell your mother." I promised and we continued on our way to the Pleasure Palace, a facility for male customers only.

Father let me join him in a glass of beer for the first time. A hostess came in to direct us to a guest room. My father said to me, "This is going to be a night of firsts for you. You have never made love to a woman before, have you?" I blushed and shook my head. As we arrived upstairs, a half-dressed woman greeted us and invited us to sit. She pulled her chair over closer to mine and said, "You're so cute; this one will be on the house."

Father said that he would wait for me downstairs but I delayed his departure. I knew what was expected of me, and I told him that I would rather not be put to the test. I couldn't adapt that quickly.

I couldn't go through with this test of my manhood. My big dread had always been having my father know about my sexuality. Father patted me on the head and reassured me that it was alright if I didn't participate. I gathered that he was not going to waste the opportunity to have a little fun. He made me promise I wouldn't tell anybody back home.

I headed for the door, but the woman's gentle gestures to come to her stopped me. I didn't want to displease anybody so I did as she requested. She caressed my cheeks again and turned to Father, "Would you mind if he watches us make love? He has to learn about it sometime."

I turned crimson and couldn't face my father. Neither of us spoke up, so she just assumed that it was agreed upon. She told me to go behind the partition screen that separated the bed from the rest of the room. I did and found a chair to sit in.

I could tell by the conversation that the couple had gone over to the bed. I just had to peek-- I couldn't help myself. I was drawn to the scene like a moth to a flame. She was lounging on the bed and father was standing beside her. Her hand was caressing him and I was shocked at the size of his erection.

I grasped my own puny specimen in shame. I was glad that all I had to do was watch instead of perform. I couldn't remain in my chair, I had to get up and peek some more. They were at it full swing and I barely had time to grab a handkerchief from my pocket so as not to soil the carpet.

I was red-faced when we said good-bye but our hostess patted my package and asked me if I learned anything that night. I was dumbstruck and didn't dare look at Father. I tipped my cap and managed a thank you as we left the room. Good old Father; he understood my feelings, so he didn't tease me about the event. He never even asked me what I thought of it all.

It wasn't until the next day that I could come up with an answer to the question that the prostitute asked me-- "Did you learn anything?" Yes! I learned that watching people fuck is a hell of a lot of fun. I sometimes think that it may have been that experience that set me firmly on the path of becoming a voyeur.

SIBLINGS

My first recollections about sex centered on my siblings. Until I was about six, I was so self-centered that I hadn't even noticed that boys were built differently from girls.

All kids like to reach under the bedcovers and rub themselves. Maybe it's an exaggeration to describe this simple touching as sexual-- "sensual" would be more accurate. The delight comes from more than pleasant sensations; part of the fun is getting away with the forbidden.

Your parents weren't likely to catch you misbehaving but God might. If you kept the covers up and didn't expose any skin, then you figured He couldn't see what's going on. Still, you wondered if maybe he had x-ray eyes and could see right through your bedcovers and even through your nightclothes. It's funny how all kids cast God in the role of being the ultimate voyeur! But didn't we learn in Sunday school that God is everywhere and sees everything?

One night my sister Lorna came into my room quietly and saw the bedclothes moving. Before I knew it, she pulled back the sheets and exposed me with penis in hand. She pointed at it and giggled; then she left. We never talked about that particular incident again. I guess Lorna was too guilty about her own activities to cast stones.

Lorna was just getting interested in sex, and since I was her best pal, she invited me to learn about it too. I remember us being nude together in the bathtub.. Lorna pointed to my little penis and said, "That's funny!" Not knowing what else to do, I said, "Yours is funny too." After we got out of the tub, she asked me if I wanted a closer look and I agreed.

She came over, took my hand, and led me to the toilet. Then she told me to sit down. After that, she stood in front of me and bent over backward so I could see her little anus. Then she turned around and bent backward so I could see her little vulva.

I was dumbstruck, but she was excited. She asked me, "Which hole do you like best?" I was too frightened to answer. I started to whimper and complain that I was afraid Mother would catch us and that Father would give me a beating. I remember reminding Lorna that, "Some fathers even cut off their boy's things when they are naughty."

She tried to comfort me, "I'll show you something else if you'll stop crying." She took my place on the toilet seat, hitched a little backward and let out a little stream of urine. Then she grabbed my hand and pulled it into the warm urine stream. I didn't quite know what was happening but I started smiling again. From that day on, I have always appreciated a chance to join in a Golden Shower with my female partners.

She sat back and pulled me closer, and told me not to be a big baby. She reached out to touch my member but I knew instinctively that it was a very bad thing to do.

She saw that her action upset me but she couldn't just ignore her awakened interest. She reached down to spread her legs and she asked me if I wanted to touch her, but I was frightened to death. She grasped my hand, dragged it over to her groin, and held it there. I whimpered until she let me go.

That should have been the last of our games but it was only the beginning. While we were getting into our nightclothes she warned me, "Now that you've touched me down there, you have to do whatever I tell you."

The next day I carried her books to school and that night I learned what she really meant by, "Doing whatever I say."

She made me take down my undershorts and stand before her awaiting her command. She told me to come closer so she could hold my thing. I told her, "No!" but she threatened to tell Mother what I made her do the previous night. I was only nine and easily intimidated, so I went over to her.

I wasn't just frightened-- I was excited at the same time. Kids love to play forbidden games. She grabbed my penis and pulled it one way and then the other so that she could have a good look. It started to get hard and that really delighted her. She started rubbing it and it got even harder. It started to feel like it might burst-- it felt too good and I became so frightened that I struggled free.

The next night she pulled me quietly into her room, and made me crawl under the covers. She reached down and touched me. She tired of that shortly, and asked if I wanted to play another game. I said, "Yes." because I wasn't too comfortable with her touching me-- it felt too good. She reached under the bedclothes and pulled off her panties, and I knew she was going to make me do something I shouldn't do.

She handed her panties to me and said, "Put them on." I obeyed, and as I did, I felt a magical glow spread from my toes up to my navel. I wanted to wear them while sleeping so that I could keep that sensation, but I was afraid Mother would come and find me dressed inappropriately. I took off the panties and handed them to her reluctantly. She put them back on and then gave me a kiss. That was the last time I had the opportunity to dally with her.

She never again offered me her panties to dress in, but I couldn't forget that experience. After a week or so I got tired of waiting, so I sneaked a pair of her panties from the dirty clothesbasket and hid them behind the storage boxes in my clothes closet. Every day I would take them down and sniff and cuddle with them for a few minutes, and then put them back.

One day I took it into my head to wear them to school. That whole day I had a mixture of feelings. On the one hand, I had my dirty little secret, thanks to my naughty sister. On the other hand, I was afraid of being caught, dressed as a girl. I had to skip physical education class and was relieved to get safely home that afternoon.

On a later day I tried bunching up the panties and putting them in my book bag to take to school. When I did that, it was as though Lorna were with me throughout the day. I still like to dress in girl's clothes, especially the articles that are worn closest to the skin. I just love braziers to pieces!

It wasn't the last time that I saw Lorna naked. From that day forth, I took every opportunity to repeat the chance of seeing her lower parts. I didn't want to touch her-- I was afraid. I just wanted to see her body. I became obsessed about girls bodies, an obsession that persists today as my chief symptom of voyeurism.

I tried to hide in Lorna's closet, but she scolded me when she found out. She suddenly became modest. Only later as an adult, did I come to realize why she stopped letting me see her body. She was pubescent and I guess she was embarrassed about her tiny titties

I sneaked over to the bathroom door and thrilled to hear the tinkle of her peeing in the toilet. Even the flush of the toilet was sexualized. The older I grew the more obsessed I became with people's things. I loved talking about sexual things with my schoolmates. I was too timid to talk dirty to the girls but if they started it, I joined in eagerly.

Sister Lorna helped me broaden my experience with girls. She knew which were the bad girls in her class-- they talked about dirty things. She offered one of them a whole dollar if she would meet up with me for a show and tell session. She agreed and we met in the field near the school.

We said hello to one another and then she asked for the dollar. I gave it to her and she came over and stood in front of me. She pulled down her panties and peed on the ground. She wanted me to do the same so I unzipped and fished around a bit, and then produced my stream obligingly.

I felt cheated. Here I was showing off my precious thing and all she did was lift her skirt and make a little puddle in the dirt. At least a guy's thing would be worth a dollar to look at. I was proud that it stood out in front of me, even though it was too puny to brag about.

When I was about 12-years-old I became bolder. I wasn't much into doing-- just sneaking around and talking about sex. I began spying on my older brother to see if he was doing the naughty thing that boys do. He was a horny teen-ager, and so eventually he provided me with plenty of interesting action to watch.

He would lie on his bed with a playboy book in one hand and himself in the other. That was the way I f learned about ejaculation first hand. (Joke intended.)

One evening I crept upstairs quietly and Brother was not in his room. I found him stretched out on Lorna's bed and she was getting him off. I scurried to my own room in puzzlement and excitement because my hand wandered down to my groin and came up sticky.

I may have just become a man but I was a frightened boy. I pulled off my undershorts and put them with the trash to be burned. Then I scrubbed down in the shower, in the hope that Mother wouldn't discover my dirty deed.

I kneeled down at my bedside and promised God that never again would I touch myself down there. Within a week I was pounding away again, but I felt very guilty about it and sought forgiveness in prayer. I was frightened to death of what Father might do if he knew. I refrained from doing myself as much as possible, but then the juices sought release during my sleep, when I couldn't control my body.

I realized that I got more pleasure from the dreams than I did from the begrudging relief I gave my system with my hand. The dreams expanded in content and beauty; my full appreciation of the female body was developing. I noticed that the night-time ejaculation didn't bring with it the strong guilt feelings of having done something bad and dirty. I couldn't be blamed if they occurred when I was asleep. It got so I couldn't wait to go to sleep and have a wet dream.

I noticed that when I masturbated every day I didn't have these delightful wet dreams. I just wanted to dream and see the exciting sexual world that lay beyond my daytime grasp. I was well along the path of becoming a dedicated voyeur; all I lacked was regressing back to spying on my siblings. I tried to behave, but my raging hormones drove me to look for sexual interests everywhere.

Alas, the old opportunities were lost in the past. Lorna locked her door and the best I could do was to hold a water glass upside down against the partition wall to hear her bumping around and groaning. I guess my siblings were too old to be able to enjoy innocent, incestuous sexual exploration. I never encountered them together again. My brother probably was getting sex outside the home. I could tell because he stopped closing his bedroom door all the time.

My sexual guilt was lessened as the novelty of masturbation wore off, I loved to look at dirty books while masturbating-- another indication that I was well along the road to becoming a "Happy Voyeur." I had trouble keeping my mind on my academic studies. I wondered if I was a sex maniac.

I should have quit those kid's games while I was ahead. Instead, as my voyeuristic needs expanded, I started spying on adults, but my motivation was different.

Children are driven by anatomic curiosity to spy on other children. My latest interest in adults was more like-- "Do grown-ups do these dirty things too? Surely, not Mom and Dad! That's disgusting!"

I persisted until I eventually caught them going at in their bedroom. I saw what I came to see, but I walked away disappointed. I felt as if I had been cheated-- as if my parents lied to me. It seemed that God was not in His Heaven meting out punishment. My brother didn't go blind from masturbation and neither did I.

I learned the truth-- all sexual prohibitions were simply obstacles to deprive us of our joys with the wave of an authoritative scepter. When I became an adult I would be free to live a deceitful life just like the rest of them.

The parental bedroom action had lessened my interest in intercourse, but that meant I had to seek gratification in sneakier ways. I may have been clever about sex when I was twelve, but I was far from the master that I would become over time. Still I made a big stride when I realized that sex is for deriving pleasure, while intercourse is for making babies.

I had such masturbatory guilt that I was 20-years-old before I could look a teacher or my father in the eye. Guilt over self-arousal is a prerequisite to becoming a proper voyeur. Voyeurism itself is a sneaky way to become aroused and blame it on the target. The disheveled, partly clad women in this world are the real cause of sin, not us poor guys with skinny, grasping fingers.

We are as blameless as the aging, jealous dowager, who complains about all girls being tramps. There is no greater manifestation of sinful interest than the vigorous protest coming from those, who most desire to be bad.

SCHOOL

I used to get in trouble with the teacher when I was still drawing stick figures with crayons. I preferred representations of men rather than animals. I would get the figure made and then add a line projecting laterally that started at the junction of the trunk line with the two legs. I still can remember the teacher's annoyance as she asked me, "What's that?" As she pointed to my projecting line I would reply, "That's just a third leg." She and I both knew it was no leg.

I didn't like school when I first enrolled; it seemed as if everybody was bigger than I was. The girls ran around giggling and making silly faces at us boys. I was still in the childhood stage, when you expect God to punish you for your dirty thoughts. I was a timid child. I guess I got that way because I was afraid that grown-ups would find out what I was doing by myself with my free time.

The activities became more interesting when I joined the upper grades at the playground. Most of the time I just watched others kids play games. The girl's gym clothes were skimpy enough so that I could catch glimpses of growing boobs-- breasts that were just large enough to get my attention and hold it. I would go into reveries that would attach bare sexual organs and curved thighs to the rest of the torso.

* * * * *

I used to ride home on the school bus, because it was too far to walk. One of my girl classmates lived at the end of the route near me. I used to sit in the seat behind her and imagine that she was clasping my little pecker in a sweaty hand.

One day I felt braver than usual because I had just found out that the teacher gave me a grade of A on a special project. I felt competent, accepted, and ready to prove that I was a man.

I tapped my classmate on the shoulder and she turned in her seat to be greeted by a tiny penis waving up at her. She laughed and pushed me back in my seat, but this attracted the attention of the male driver. Nobody said anything and I arrived alone at the last stop.

The driver reached out and grabbed me by the shoulder as I walked up front to get off. He pulled me toward him with one hand and he grabbed his own big crotch with the other. He said half gruffly and half amused, "Wait until you have something worthwhile down there before you go showing it off!" I was afraid he was going to take out his own penis to humiliate me. Even soft, his would put my little hard one to shame. As he let me go, he warned me, "If I ever catch you doing that again on my bus I'll take you straight to the principal."

I was intimidated and never waved my goodies on that bus again. I lived in fear for the next couple of days, waiting for the principal or my parents to summon me. Nothing came of it except that my efforts to be more sexually aggressive were discouraged. I think that unhappy experience may have put me off exhibitionism, and redirected me toward voyeurism.

Upper-grade recesses became more interesting, and I even looked forward to going to school-- it was because of June, mostly. I was standing next to her one day and got a sniff of her body odor mixed with the shampoo she used in her hair. Heaven opened up for me. I sidled up closer to sniff her hair. I positioned myself over her shoulder as if I were about to devour it or any part of her I could reach.

She made a partial turn, and I was terrified that she might be repelled, and complain to the teacher. At that moment I thought, "My God! She can tell what I'm thinking, what I'm doing."

An angelic look dispelled my panic as she broke out into a smile. She said, "You're Abraham aren't you? Your sister is a friend of mine." Of course I was dumbstruck and couldn't talk. I smiled and walked away from my own true love.

After that encounter I felt more confident when standing behind a girl; I would sidle up to any with budding tits. I spent my time ranking the girls I had studied and sniffed, but I never found one as lovely as June.

One other time, I almost built up the nerve to go over and talk to June. I prayed that my true intentions wouldn't be apparent. I tripped clumsily as I approached her, and I brushed a firm little boob as I put out my hand to keep from falling. I felt the magic of sexual stimulation throughout my body. I swore I would never wash the hand that had the honor of touching her breast.

I knew what my evil desires were and I was ashamed of them. Yes, I wanted to see her breast exposed and perhaps, be allowed to touch it briefly. To lick it or to suck it was far beyond any expectation. Sadly, I was too shy even to talk to her again. I went home and lay in my bed thinking about her. I had to collect myself and go downstairs for dinner or Mother might divine the source of the smile on my face.

I learned a very important lesson-- "There is more joy in anticipation than in actually acquiring that which is desired." The desired, might have been the perfume of an apple pie that was waiting to come out of the oven, or it might have been the surrender of a damsel. It was neither of those; my lesson came from waiting for an amazing gadget to arrive in the mail. It was a pair of magic x-ray spectacles.

I was the happiest kid in the block because I had ordered a pair of x-ray spectacles by mail. I would be able to see through dresses and even thick braziers! I could wear them innocently in the schoolyard and see under all the girls' clothes. What should have been the climax of my life turned out to be a hoax.

The device was made of cardboard and produced an optical illusion. It failed to give me the feeling of omnipotence that I expected to enjoy. Instead, I had an empty feeling in the pit of my stomach as I realized what a sucker I was.

From that time on I was less eager to seek the real thing-- I would settle for copies or castoffs-- I was content to borrow instead of to own. I never was a collector-- I was content to sit back and watch other people enjoy their possessions. At the same time I realized that the sexual objects I desired were largely illusory.

* * * * *

I'm going to share with you something I have never been able to talk about with anyone else-- I'm too ashamed. I used to sneak quietly into the bathroom while my mother was showering. I could see her silhouette through the flimsy curtain and it exited me.

I tried to masturbate while watching her, but I couldn't keep it hard, because I felt so naughty. I was not only "abusing" myself but also, disrespecting my mother. As I got older I tried it a couple of more times with better success. I was learning that guilt about sex is for children, not for adults. At the same time my hormones were blasting to a new high level.

Nonetheless, I made a serious decision that day-- I would never marry anyone like my mother. I realized that I wanted a mate to cuddle with, but I would never be able to do naughty things with the mother of my children. Yes! I had a full-blown Oedipus Complex.

* * * * *

As a teen-ager, I found satisfaction for my lust with male school chums because it was convenient, but that didn't continue long. Throughout my exploratory years I was dedicated to seeking out the female body and the promise of release from my crude maleness.

It's too bad that our society doesn't supply girls to the adolescent male, struggling with self-doubts. Such a regime would produce men, sure of themselves and ready to face obstacles. Instead, society uses guilt and ignorance to conceal the finest aspect of life-- sex! I wouldn't go far enough to say that God delights in creating men with polymorphic sexual perversions, but I do suspect Him of enjoying the resulting confusion.

* * * * *

By mere chance I caught one of my schoolmates with his head pressed against the changing room wall of the girl's gym. He concealed his right hand and what was in it, so I suspected that he was up to dirty tricks. As he left his face was crimson, so I realized that I had hit a mother lode. I took his place and saw two girls changing from their gym clothes into their swimming suits. They had to disrobe completely!

Anything so delightful and exciting had to be sinful. I was only a kid and had a child's perspective. An adult would have seen the situation as improper but understandable, but not me. I knew that I was destined to go to Hell, but I had the balls to do so with a smile on my face-- I was growing up. I returned quite often to peep through that knothole.

My guilt feelings over sexual interests were rapidly being replaced with a joy for life and its promises. My outlook became positive and my opportunities to engage with girls grew. I almost became a ladies man in high school.

We schoolmates succeeded in dropping our childish sexual timidity by the time we were old enough to go to the prom. We met in cars and pleasured one another in ways that eliminated the risk of pregnancy. As long as we had hands and mouths, we were content to leave copulation to the stodgy grow-ups.

I was dating all kinds of girls; I wasn't fussy. All I was looking for was someone to explore my sexuality with. The date didn't have to be pretty but she had to have a soft, curvy body. I kind of despised the skinny little girls of my age and tried to hang out more with the older girls, who had started to fill out in the right places.

I preferred obese girls-- the chubbier the better. Competition for their attention was less and they were grateful for any pleasantries they received. Many were ready to buy a guy's attention with their charms. That worked for me.

On one occasion a tubby girl exposed herself completely to me in order to bind me to her with the exchange of secrets. I should have found her blubber a nuisance because it hid her sexual parts. Being a voyeur, I was happiest just looking. I loved her chubby body and caressed it without having to deal with its vulgarities.

I often wondered about my peculiar preferences. Only when I was an adult did I realized that I was basically a voyeur and that my sexual pleasures would come from pursuing my target at a distance. I was content with being allowed just to share the same world with those lovely substantial creatures.

* * * * *

I reached the age of 20 before I was called to a man's duties. It happened quite by chance. Mother's youngest sister had just lost her husband. They were a happy couple, so my Aunt Ellie was devastated by his death. She was starved for both affection and sex.

She was staying with us for the whole summer and she had nothing to do except dote on me. I loved the attention and I have to admit that I loved the hugging too. She was only 30 and in the prime of her life. She complained about how lonely she was, and she whispered in my ear, "If only you were a man!"

Mother went to the hospital to have her appendix removed and that left Aunt Ellie and me to our own devices. On the second day, she came into my bedroom without knocking. I was devastated because she caught me lying on the bed looking at a dirty magazine.

She smiled gently as she came over to the bed and asked me what I was reading. She took the magazine from my hand, and I grew totally crimson. I looked up at her, my eyes pleading for mercy. Instead of being angry with me, she looked at my groin to see what I was hiding.

She reassured me that it was alright for boys to experiment with sex, as I was doing. She reached over and hugged me reassuringly. I wanted her embrace so desperately but I was ashamed of my erection. The tighter she held me against her breasts, the harder I became. The stiffer I got, the more uncomfortable I was.

Aunt Ellie knew just what to do. She pulled aside the sheet and looked down on my shame. To reassure me she purred, "Oh my! You're quite the man aren't you?" I couldn't answer her because of my embarrassment but that didn't stop her.

She knew what a young stud needed to learn from an older woman. She said, "It's time you had the opportunity to study all about women, and I'm going to give you that chance." I sat up staring as she took off all her clothes and climbed into bed with me. My wildest dreams were coming true.

She embraced me and I was on fire from the touch of her breast against my chest. She pinched a nipple,

"Do you like my breasts? Wouldn't you like to touch them? You can do anything you want to with me. I'm here to teach you about sex."

She guided my hand to her breast. I couldn't believe my good fortune-- I held in my hands the most precious thing in the world. I tried to concentrate on that marvelous experience, but all I could think of was my throbbing dick. I was afraid that she would feel it poking up against her and that it would repel her.

She completed the seduction by pulling me closer to her. I stopped resisting and one of her nipples slid into my mouth. She pulled back the covers some more and peeked. She said, "It looks like you like my breasts!" I didn't know what to say or what to do, so I kept on sucking. She just lay back and moaned.

I couldn't help what happened; I didn't know what was going on. My whole body convulsed as it went into a totally teeth-shaking orgasm. I was wondering if she thought masturbation was a deadly sin. It looked like she had her doubts about the validity of that teaching. She even seemed to like cleaning me up.

We lay there naked, and I found that my embarrassment was replaced with curiosity and an excited interest. I knew she would understand, so I shared my deepest secrets with her.

I told her how I felt guilty about masturbating and how I could avoid it for a week or more but finally would succumb to temptation. She laughed at me and told me, "Sex is such fun that you should enjoy it every day!" I was hearing the real truth from an adult for the first time.

She encouraged me to give myself over completely to pleasure. I did so with great joy and gladness. From then on when I was bothered by guilt feelings, I just recalled that liberating experience and proceeded to enjoy whatever naughty thing I was doing.

She rolled over on her back to expose herself and she pressed my cheek against her belly so that I had to look straight into her groin area. I saw close up for the first time what I had been catching glimpses of during my voyeuristic escapades. Aunt Ellie asked nothing of me. She just lay there so I could peek and poke.

She had a smile of contentment on her face because she seldom found such an appreciative partner. All my reluctance had disappeared and I was ready for anything. After a while she asked me, "Don't you want to enter me like a boy and come out like a man?" I was awkward but I did my duty.

That day would never be repeated-- it couldn't be. It was the day I became a man. I learned later that she was what people call an exhibitionist, and even had been arrested for driving around topless in her convertible.

JONATHAN P. SLOW

TREATMENT FACILITY

I avoided suffering the indignities of prison life by going to a state hospital, but I landed in the state nut house which could be a worse plight. Not only did I have no fixed release date, I was subjected to the whims of incompetent professional staff and officials. The classic description of conditions in London's 19th century Bedlam Hospital sounded like those still found in one of our typical state mental hospitals.

Dr. Sol Hororwitz, the superintendent, was a washed-up political appointee, who had delivered up enough of his barbequing friends to the political party to merit his appointment as the "Boss." Prior to becoming *Acting* Superintendent, he was in private practice. The Governor was afraid of newspaper diatribes if he converted Sol Hororwitz's position to Superintendent, with the permanence that is implied by the title.

Newspaper editorials about malpractice charges against Dr. Hororwitz were rather embarrassing. The plaintiff had a roomful of witnesses to testify to Dr. Hororwitz's incompetent handling of a routine operation. It was disclosed that the patient almost bled-out in surgery when Dr. Hororwitz panicked, and his assistant had to take charge to close up the patient. The patient asked for five million dollars. He was awarded that, plus another five million penalty for Dr. Hororwitz's gross negligence in performing his duties.

Dr. Hororwitz's friends no longer answered his phone calls after the disastrous outcome of the trial. We can assume that he had some dirt on a high-ranking party member because the Governor approved his appointment.

Dr. Sol Hororwitz had to search far and wide to find professionals and staff. He was careful to hire only worn-out, beaten-down professionals. He deliberately chose applicants, who were too stupid to be capable of rebelling against his mismanagement and, who were incapable of establishing their own regime of incompetence. His staff could see through the Boss but they had nowhere else to go. They kept their mouths shut and stumbled along, grateful for receiving even a small income in their well-paid profession.

His Director of the Infirmary was typical. He was a proper-appearing physician, who claimed that his tuberculosis limited his capacity to hold a full-time job. Actually, he was a bipolar psychotic in partial remission from time-to-time. Some of the time he went around raving like a mad man. He would suddenly pop a couple of his own prescribed barbiturate pills, and exit from the real world.

His bar hopping and alcohol kept him strung out for days. A week later he would reappear with the explanation that he had needed a rest from the stress of his work. There were no blood tests for drugs required at the time. The high concentration of barbiturates, amphetamine, or cocaine kept him excitable but that was ignored. There was nobody with even minimum qualifications to replace him during his absences. Later I learned that he was an M.D. who lost his licence to practice medicine in Massachusetts. The State Board disciplined him for abuse of prescription drugs and endangering a patient.

He always was reemployed when he returned from a bender because no more than one or two patients died from his neglect. Voters were never enthusiastic about funding the hospital, so the Superintendent had to hire applicants, who met sub-minimal standards. The legislators were not ready to allocate $100,000.00 a year per patient, as they did for the University Hospital.

The professional staff covered one another's asses so that problems wouldn't surface that the Superintendent would have to deal with. The Boss found it expedient to appoint their Director of the Infirmary to the post of Pathologist and local Medical Examiner. They were able to bury everybody's mistakes.

The Boss had a professional staff of Director, Assistant, Supervisor of Services, a Psychologist, and Head of Nursing care, and three derelict physicians. What a gang! I could tell you about them but you wouldn't believe that such a collection of incompetents could exist inside or outside a hospital.

Well, as a matter of fact, some did have to change status from time to time and become patients. Still, I should be the first to point out that marginal people still can contribute to our society. I was a good example. I was a helpful young Graduate Assistant with a positive impact, despite my psychological problems.

Similarly, the Director of the Infirmary was able to make his contribution to society most of the time, but none of us is perfect. We all have our disabilities. Which of you male readers can ignore completely the flash of pink panties or a lacy brassiere, even if they are just hanging on the wash line? "Let he who is without blame cast the first stone!"

One day I was walking through a treatment room where electric convulsive therapy was about to be administered to a middle-aged woman with a terrified look on her face. The doctor was talking to her. I'll never know where Dr. Hororwitz found such a particularly nasty physician!

He grabbed me by the arm to detain me as I passed by. He dragged me over to the woman's bedside and announced to her, "Now I'm going to electrocute you!" He became more expansive, "And you fellow! I'll electrocute you too if you don't obey orders."

The announcement was followed by a sharp zap and the patient bounced around in the bed with clonic seizures. Of course, after she woke up she had forgotten the frightening threats, but the rest of us, who were at her bedside, still remembered.

The hospital was a straight-out expense from the taxpayers' pockets. The least the State could do was employ their own handicapped, who would otherwise draw disability benefits without doing any work. The digital age had not yet penetrated the gloom of the dusky hospital environment. Incoming phone calls still were routed over cables by the hospital switchboard operator.

It was my good fortune to befriend one of the handicapped switchboard operators. She was blind from birth but that didn't diminish her passion to learn about the world. She was 30 years old and had never been laid. In fact, she never had touched a naked penis, even by accident. She had rubbed up against a few in a crowded bus or a ticket cue, but she never had the chance to unzip obstructive trousers.

I used to go over to her station and sweet talk her whenever I was in the administrative center. She was reasonably attractive, so it wasn't hard to be pleasant to her. I told her about my voyeuristic obsessions and she obliged me by pulling down the front of her peasant blouse to the nipple line.

I wanted to be nice to her and-- OK, my own impulses propelled me, too. I moved closer to her switchboard console, rather out-of-sight of any passer-by. As we talked, I noticed two things, first her breath started coming in gasps, and second, her skirt kept rising higher and higher. Then, I almost lost control when I also saw a pink nipple peeking out at me.

As I pressed my concealed penis against her shoulder, she emitted squeaks of delight. I in turn, became very excited and couldn't resist the temptation to expand her limited sexual knowledge. I loved it when she took the initiative-- she popped it out of its hiding place and stroked it.

She looked up at me with pleading eyes that could not see, and she begged me, "Please don't think badly of me. I'm blind but I'm just as alive as any other girl you let do this to you." My response was a slow moan as I let her have her way.

On future visits to her desk, I managed to get around the side and under her console far enough to prevent passers-by from noticing me. She never asked anything of me; she was grateful for the few crumbs she was receiving, and she showed it.

I liked to think that our experiences together encouraged her to browse around to find others who could meet her needs. I'm a selfish bastard. I couldn't be bothered about her welfare. I only cared about increasing my own sources of gratification.

* * * * *

The Superintendent was married with children, but so are a lot of people. The existence of children doesn't seem to limit people's extra-marital games very much. It never even occurred to me that the Superintendent's wife might be able to keep him happy under the sheets.

Who was doing the Superintendent? It was hard to gather information about his life because I never had been in his apartment or his office. I was forced to rely upon the gossip method of proof.

His housekeeper seemed a bit too old to attract him, but age is no determinant as to how much pleasure a person can provide another. The nanny was a better prospect but the boss' wife always seemed to be present in the apartment, and she seldom left the hospital.

I tried to gather information about the Superintendent's movements outside the hospital. His chauffeur drove him to his various appointments during the day, but I couldn't get any specifics. There was little else to occupy me, so I continued to probe.

I went a step deeper in my investigation. I befriended his driver in the hope that he would reveal something about the Boss' movements. I kept thinking that the driver would be the key, because he would be taking him to those rendezvous. I was both right and wrong at the same time.

One day when I was chatting with the driver, he reached over and clasped my thigh. He asked me, "Don't you want to slip off with me and have a little fun?" His intent was clear. I told him, thanks but that I was afraid we would be caught. He smiled up at me coyly and said, "I've got the key to the Super's garage. We go there all the time so I know that it's safe." I didn't need him anymore, so I thanked him for the offer and avoided him in the future.

Doc Walters was one of three staff physicians. One of those physicians was a fairly competent so he was able to clean up Dr. Walters' messes. Dr. Walters couldn't tell shit from Shinola but he did have an M.D. degree. He obtained it even though he must have been absent from a lot of classes to remain so ignorant in his field.

Dr. Walters was so old that his tremors made his written signature illegible. His trailing M.D. was still recognizable and that was all he was needed for. His level of professionalism was demonstrated by his presentation of a patient to a staff meeting: "Diagnosis: Psychopathic Personality caused by Alcoholism." And those are the places that the courts send us for assistance!

It is no easy thing to leave it up to idiots to determine your future. At least I had my blind telephone operator for pleasant distractions .To survive the six months would require patience, optimism, and considerable self-confidence. Somehow, everything always worked out for me over time.

* * * * *

The constrictions of an institution limited my capacity to enjoy perverted sexual practices. That doesn't mean that I was sexually inactive because opportunities did abound. I am too needy and too indulgent to settle for simple self-gratification. There was little else of interest there to occupy me, but I had to be careful to maintain my Jekyll and Hyde act.

I had to play the role of the repentant sinner so that I could get back to my old ways as soon as possible. It was easy enough for me to be likable; I just let my good nature show. My extensive experience at lying to cover up my mischievous adventures prepared me for keeping the hospital authorities in the dark. Eventually I managed to earn early release with my pleasant manner, lying tongue, and good record.

I had to hide away everything sexual in my life or it would expose my duplicity. When I asked to be given duty in the infirmary, the officials assumed that I was being a repentant Christian.

My real reasons were quite different. Doctor and Nurses games always fascinated me. Perhaps it was because of the power to help others that is bestowed on caretakers. Bullshit! What really turned me on was looking at partially clothed bodies.

Working the infirmary gave me the chance to bathe partially clothed men. I would have preferred that they were women but I had no choice. I was both amused and excited by men's attempts to hide half-erect penises.

Some of my special patients smiled when they saw me coming on the ward. They were just a few younger patients, who were pleasant and agreeable. I took enough time bathing them to give them hand jobs.

Sometimes the whole encounter at work transcended a mundane sex-organ focus. By now you know that I'm not talking about just satisfying the soul. The most satisfaction I could obtain came from half exposing a bared mound of the body for an injection. I loved to shoot the stream into a shoulder, but grasping a rump and penetrating it with my needle was even better. The needle gave me a feeling of power that made me omnipotent. I was in charge for that moment. I wished I really was God, then nobody could take me to task for my indiscretions.

As I pressed my needle into hot flesh, I would experience a hot flash of emotion surge through my body. It was like a genital orgasm that had been dispersed throughout my whole body. I missed that thrill when I was transferred to another job a few weeks later. I knew I would have to replace my infirmary kicks with some even sneakier pleasure.

As I completed the day's duty in the infirmary, I would remember my childhood aspiration. I dreamed of being a plastic surgeon, who spent his days improving the curvature of those already-beautiful adornments. Some guys have all the luck!

My assignment to the infirmary was short-lived because I liked it. We were not in the hospital to be amused or entertained; if we were enjoying our stay then something was wrong.

They transferred me to the library. It could have been worse. I got to substitute National Geographic pictures of Uganda titty parades for the real flesh of the sick ward. Maybe I missed something. This move forced me to regress back to cherishing forbidden National Geographic nudies. That was supposed to be treatment?

* * * * *

People view all sexual desires as if they were something acquired voluntarily, that should be renounced. These views are rooted in the old days when religion attributed mental illness to possession by the Devil. The medical view is not much different—"Sexual impulses are symptoms that should be healed."

Hospital officials, and even the professionals, pretended that my sexual urges would disappear magically. They completely ignored all their own personal sexual impulses that they gratified regularly. Had I consented to a visit from the priest, I'm sure he would have told me that all I had to do was put my faith in Jesus and the temptations would disappear.

In the meantime I had to make the best of what I had. My girlfriend Bunny didn't care much whether my confederate was male or female, just as long as I continued to support her in our respectable community. She knew that I would come back to her bed, once I was released from custody.

There wasn't much of a selection of inmates, who would be suitable companions for me. They were all a rough lot, so it was difficult to find a partner, who I would be able to identify with. In effect, I had to seek out the "Prettiest goat on the island."

Roy came into my life and my luck changed. Roy was a pleasant 40-year-old man with complex sexual urges. He would be hard to label because of the lack of focus that characterized his sexual life. He was not aggressive-- just friendly. I recognized him as a good mate right from the start, but I moved cautiously. I had to be sure that he was trustworthy and that he would not disclose our contacts.

I liked Roy's easy-going manner. He used to say, "It's people like us, who give sex a bad name!" He didn't crowd or rush me. We started hanging out together, smoking and playing games. Only two days passed before we exchanged the salient points in our histories.

It turned out that he was hospitalized as a sexual offender, too. Only a few days more went by before he revealed that he had targeted me because he knew that I was there for sexual misconduct. So you can see that my luck really was turning.

Roy was sent up for soliciting guys in the city park. He explained that he liked everything about sex and didn't have strong preferences. Roy said he had worked the park for more than a year with considerable success. He told me that one of his attractive prospects proved to be a big disappointment when the cop reached into his pocket and pulled out a shield instead of a fleshy play toy.

Given his choice, Roy would prefer to receive a blowjob, but he liked to give them too. He knew that it is easier for guys to accept the donor part of the action, so he asked likely prospects if he could do them. He asked for nothing in return-- at least not on the first contact.

Roy loved the game and was good at it. When guys came back for a repeat, Roy would ask them to perform on him. A few did and they became weekly companions, while the reluctant ones found themselves left out. He regretted that his greediness lead him to stray from his regular mates and get busted by an undercover cop.

Roy was married but he had no children. He was an electrical contractor and made a good living when he was free to work. His wife couldn't endure his earlier incarcerations so she divorced him.

Our society is so uncomfortable about sex that it puts a label on everybody. They would label Roy a homosexual and me too, even though I admire the female body much more. Once you engage in a heterosexual act you lose society's approval and you get pegged unfairly as being gay.

Roy was more than my sex toy; we became very close friends. He admired me because of what I am-- a successful, educated man, who indulges his sexual impulses with prudence. I developed real feelings for him during the six months we spent locked up together. I couldn't imagine us living separately after our release.

Were my feelings for Roy those of love or did I just like the guy? Maybe I was just reluctant to give up a good sex machine. I had never wondered much about my sexual orientation before because I never had such a close male friend. Now I had to wonder. "Was I a homosexual all along and didn't recognize it? As the joke goes, maybe I just, "Got sucked into it."

Our close relationship was not unusual for two male lovers. We were soul mates, not just eager receptacles for each other's sperm. I felt what he sensed and he experienced my own gratifications. We exchanged bodies when we were at the peak of passion. I experienced his orgasms by being absorbed by him-- by becoming a part of him. His joy and his sadness became mine. We dedicated ourselves to each other because there was nothing else in our daily life that mattered.

We became so close that we could talk about anything, so I told him that I was afraid that I had fallen in love with him. He replied, "Who the fuck cares as long as we're happy together! Call us homosexual or supermen-- whatever you want. It won't affect our relationship."

I loved Roy's straight, pragmatic approach to life. We embraced and promised not to let the parole officers ever separate us.

The ward was loaded with sex-starved inmates. Most of them took care of their own needs and never hooked up with other inmates. Everybody would get his own happy hour after lights went out, except for some of the withdrawn schizophrenics. We weren't allowed to read in bed, so masturbation became a refuge from boredom.

Every so often at night, a deep moan would slip out from one of the cells.

The voyeur in just about everybody makes sexy magazines attractive. We would have preferred to have hard-core porno videos but had to settle for magazines with titillating nudes. Playboy magazines were allowed and every inmate had at least one under his pillow, waiting to welcome him home from work.

Hard-core magazines were worth their weight in gold. Only a few remained in circulation because they were easily found and confiscated. Our attendants took the porno magazines back home to their residences to enliven their sex lives. A stupid public acted as if we would be morally misguided by such printed material. Society wears the blinders of an old horse.

During the daylight hours, some of the braver souls would risk punishment so they could enjoy a few minutes of sexual pleasure with a partner. It was a risky business because there were no really private places to join bodies. Furthermore, you needed a third party to stand guard because the participants would be too busy to keep watch for approaching attendants. Using a watchperson is risky in itself, because it provides fuel for a gossiping mouth. If the attendants caught a pair in action, then a reprimand would be placed in each record for all to see at their release hearings.

Roy and I were locked up in separate cells so we couldn't team up for sexual activities. Since I am a voyeur, I prefer more gentle sex action that involves looking even more than touching. About once a week, each of us would hold up a mirror so that the bars of the neighboring cell were reflected. Anything protruding through the bars to the walkway would be clearly visible. It is unnecessary to explain what each of us held in the other hand.

The good thing about having a polymorphic sexuality is that you have many avenues available to provide satisfaction. Guys like us always can find something of interest in an institution where normal sex is unavailable,

Roy and I had another game…

After lights out, we would crawl into bed and pull off our shorts. By previous arrangement, we would go to the grating of the other's cell and exchange shorts. Back in bed, we could love on the underwear and even dress in it. As the excitement rose, each of us would lay the shorts on the bed and climb on top of them.

The dim light of the cell cast enough shadows to allow us to imagine all sorts of things. We would see our lover's body, his face, and his fingers as though reaching out to touch our own. Both of us populated our misty worlds according to his own needs. At the peak of excitement, relief came with little extra effort.

You can use your own imagination to picture the sexual activities that went on around us. Guys were getting gratification in every way possible. I hesitate to describe the details; I don't want to bore you or annoy you with the grossness of it all. Neither do you want to hear about the routine details of our institutionalized life.

Let's just skip on to the special kinky thing we looked forward to on visitor's day. My new girlfriend Bunny was supportive throughout my trouble. She never really understood me but she was there. I really looked forward to seeing her on visitors' day-- and I do mean, "Seeing her!"

Bunny needed the moral support of her girlfriend and roommate Kitty, in order to go through with such crude exhibitionism. The two of them would drive out together for a visit-- to reward their guys for being patient.

They took adjacent visiting booths and started the visit by slumping down in their chairs with their skirts sliding up slowly. Neither of them wore panties. Each of us got a big eyeful that would have to keep us going the rest of the month.

Then as a special treat, the girls switched places so that the other guy would be inspired by the sight of strange pussy. Both of us went nuts and wanted to get back to our cells so we could get some relief. The girls giggled because they loved teasing us.

The guards knew what was going on but there was no reason for them to interfere. Sometimes an attendant would disappear for a few minutes, and the sheepish grin on his face betrayed him when he returned. On the way back to our cells, Roy whispered to me, "If they only knew how much fun I was having, they'd turn me loose!"

Roy and I were lucky to have girls, who enjoyed life and weren't so rigid that they found our perverted pleasures unbearable. We looked forward to the time when we could party together on the outside. My first marriage lacked all this kind of excitement, and sex itself became boring. At least Maureen was a good mother and provided a stable home for our daughter Annie.

Unlike ex-prisoners, we were viewed as recovering mental cases, not criminals. We were exempt from the rule that prisoners on parole were forbidden to maintain contact with known ex-prisoners. We would be able to determine how we worked and where we lived, once we were released. We promised each other that we would try to arrange to live together. I offered to take him into my home and share it with him. We were regular asshole buddies.

JONATHAN P. SLOW

The six months I spent in the hospital were really worthwhile, thanks to my companion Roy and a psychologist named Jonathan P. Slow. A week after admission I met Jonathan for the first time. We hit it off right from the first.

I was resigned to being plagued with a physician, who was wholly untrained to practice in the mental health area. I expected to find a "therapist" in the chair opposite me with a slight knowledge of the human body and even less about the mind.

Those interviews that are supposed to be therapeutic are conducted under a court mandate. An incompetent professional tells you what is wrong with your life and gives you bad advice on how to fix it. They call it therapy!

Jonathan wasn't like that at all. He was young and interested in others. He dropped out of his PhD program in Clinical Psychology to earn a living, necessitated by the advent of unplanned fatherhood. With a new baby to care for, his wife was no longer able to contribute her earnings to the family upkeep. His own salary was meager, since he could not qualify for a good job until he completed the doctorate.

Nonetheless, Jonathan was determined to perform like a professional-- to take pride in his work. He didn't feel sorry for himself; to the contrary, he was grateful for the opportunity to work intensively with a few select patients.

By the middle of the first session I leaned back with relief and I even smiled at my adversary. After several sessions he told me that he felt fortunate to be able to enter a relationship with a man with my experience and understanding. I believe he meant it when he said, "I get so much out of our exchanges in sessions that I feel that you should be the therapist and I the patient." Jonathan wasn't above passing out an occasional compliment, but I knew that he was just being honest, that time.

Jonathan made it clear to me from the start that he understood the template of our relationship. He explained:

> "I realize that you are compelled to come to the sessions and vomit up some bullshit so we can go through the semblance of remediation. If we don't get to hate each other too much, then I will be ready to submit a report approving your discharge."

He told me quite frankly:

> "We can keep on thrusting and parrying for several weeks of interesting social interaction and then terminate the work amicably. But it would be a shame to waste our time together that way. We are both intelligent people and could learn a lot from each other."

I asked him "What protection do I have that revealed secrets won't go in my record and be used against me?" He gave me one of those big smiles that he held in reserve to preface one of his wise-ass comments.

"It's up to you to get me on your side through openness and a desire for understanding. Once we are friends I will want to protect you. Who knows, I might even be ready to lie for you to conceal your blemishes."

We became comfortable with each other almost from the start, and we developed mutual respect. I had been unloading to him about my childhood and he was very pleased at how things were going. I accepted the visits as an opportunity to come to know myself better and thereby improve my life. I had a feeling that my experience would be a valuable one.

One morning he told me,

"I'm going to tell you something that could cost me my job if it became general knowledge." I told him to go ahead, that his secret would be safe with me. He asked me what I thought about his new assistant that had been at the hospital for about a month. I screwed up my face into a grimace, but I didn't know what to say. He waited a short while for my answer, and then broke out into a tirade, "He's an arrogant, stupid bastard, isn't he?"

I agreed with him and he continued…

> "I can't imagine how he managed to get a PhD. He didn't learn shit, but he thinks he should go around telling people how to do their business. He's as green as can be. The only experience he ever had was a three-month internship in an institution like ours."

I let him continue,

> "He thinks that he can get my job because he has the academic qualifications. He's one of those hasty hires that you regret at length. His references were glowing so we should have realized that his last employer was trying to dump him."

I asked him, "OK, so what's the big secret?" He said with a conspirator's evil smile and chuckle…

> "I put a classified ad in the newspaper that offered all of home furnishings for sale. I indicated urgency and enclosed the address for viewing his possessions. I added that sacrifice prices were in effect because he had to move out in three days.
>
> His wife was sick at home with the measles, so she got pestered with visitors. She couldn't stay in bed like the doctor ordered. It served her right for marrying that stupid bastard of a husband. Her offense against the world of giving

birth to three of his squalling brats was unforgivable"

We both enjoyed this disclosure of his naughty escapade. He said that the Superintendent was furious about the incident and ordered an investigation by the security personnel. After several days, nothing was discovered, so the fuss subsided. Jonathan told me that the Medical Director agreed that, "It serves that intolerable prick right! I hope he takes the hint and looks for a job somewhere else." He did!

* * * * *

I learned that a saintly old man giving kindly advice is not psychotherapy. I also learned that therapy can be successful only when the couch is a classroom in which human relationships are explored. The couch is not a ping pong court for battimg words back and forth.

There are three essential prerequisites needed to open the door of progress:

The beginning point is to realize that the human mind is a *tabula rasa* with respect to interrelationships. You start life without emotional bonds, so you have to continue developing them throughout life.

Secondly, through repetitious learning in therapy you can understand how your relationships were acquired. It is also important to recognize that the earlier learning experiences affect your future perceptions.

Childhood circumstances will affect your whole adult life.

Another mantra acknowledges that learning of relationships takes place only when reinforced with reward or punishment. (When there is approval and disapproval by someone important to you like a counselor.)

* * * * *

Simplifying the complexity of relationships comes through examining emotional attachments at their simplest and crudest level. When I entered Jonathan's office the first thing I noticed about him was the bulge his penis made in his trousers. It was large enough to be interesting and it was tucked sideways coyly, as if it were waiting to be awakened. This gave an appealing curved shape to his manhood. As I sat down I wondered if he noticed my bulge too.

We all tend to notice one another's bulges but pretend not to see them, even to ourselves. It's just like two guys peeing side-by-side at a urinal-- each pretends he is all alone.

It was a few weeks before I could discuss the significance of this first meeting with Jonathan. It was important that we develop the habit of exploring everything freely. It's the little things from our formative years that enable us to react to more complex things in the future. "As the building is founded, so shall it lean."

My obscene interest in Jonathan's private parts were the beginning of my healthy interest in him as a person. I had never seen him before, but now I would sense a connection because his hidden joy became a signpost. His concealed penis was like an icon on a computer screen-- it displays little but can hide masses of information.

It's the funny little things like this that have to be followed up in therapy to make sense of the larger picture. All of us have spent a lifetime learning to repress embarrassing matters. In therapy I had to learn how to open my eyes, psychologically. Only by exploring these bunny trails can you break out into the light.

Most people are under the misapprehension that psychotherapy consists of passing words back and forth. The patriarchal nature of the therapist is to offer a few words of advice so that he can get on with his life. Good therapists and cooperative patients realize that the feelings passed back and forth between them are what is really important, not the verbal garbage.

Psychoanalytic psychotherapy recognizes full well that no changes will occur during therapy unless the patient is buffeted by mixed feelings toward the therapist. Feelings and relationships in both directions have to be examined constantly. The patient's behavior will affect the therapist just as surely as the therapist's reactions will affect the patient.

The therapist must have enough self-understanding to be able to reveal himself and enter actively into the relationship. He knows that patients, "Fall in love" with the therapist, but he must maintain some control over how he deals with their relationship.

The patient's, "Feelings of high personal regard" have to be strong enough to desire and welcome the therapist's personal approval and admiration. You can't be rewarded with a therapist's acceptance unless you care about him.

You probably know that the feelings of affection toward the therapist are given the label "Transference." The word "love" is vague and carries too much baggage. The patient will find it less threatening to accept his feelings toward a same-sex therapist, if the relationship is not described as homosexual. The feelings are what count and any reaction to the labels provides the opportunity to explore the patient's misperceptions about himself.

For instance, I told Jonathan that when I first met him I noticed his penis bulge, and that I was attracted to it. Jonathan accepted that and encouraged me to consider that "nonsense" more fully-- to follow the bunny trail.

Both he and I knew that I could have dismissed my interest as just voyeuristic. Instead of passing it off with a jingoistic term we went right to the underlying motives and impulses. I saw that my interest in his penis could be explained as a learned reaction to happy experiences with a lifetime of penises, especially my own.

We could have kept the analysis at that level but in therapy it is important to keep probing deeper. A few minutes later I came to realize that my interest really was a deeper one. I wanted the acceptance and approval of the therapist. His penis is very personal and access to it would reassure me of his acceptance of me as a friend.

From that starting point, we dug deeper. I came to see my lifetime of sexual activities as efforts to be close to others, but holding back enough so that I would stay safe. We went on to examine my ways of dealing with other threats and understanding my unique ways of defending myself.

Understandings like these can be deceptive. They can be summarized briefly in a few words, but the real impetus for change takes months and years to become consolidated. The many hours spent together in therapy are necessary to provide the motivation to bring about change through self-understanding.

Glib words of psychobabble or even good advice may affect immediate behavior, but the necessary changes will not have occurred inside. It's like removing cancerous skin-- the putrefying process continues internally but remains unnoticed.

While rubrics explain nothing, sometimes they can be useful as a way of summarizing a complex of other things. Jonathan Slow's understanding about voyeurism is reducible to "Seeking reassurance about the body and dealing with your needs."

Our needs begin in early childhood and the defences against disappointment and loss of love develop throughout childhood. Those defences against loss appear as rigid symptoms in the hospitalized neurotic patient. The psychologist views the criminal actions of the voyeur as expressions of neurotic symptoms.

When symptoms are viewed dynamically, we see that two diagnostic labels sometimes apply to the same individual. The distinction under law is clear between a voyeur and an exhibitionist, and they also are distinct psychiatric categories. However, forcing a patient to fit a label leads to blocked, categorical thinking—"He must be one or the other." Actually, the voyeur usually is both an exhibitionist, and voyeur. Psychology, like its name suggests, is not logical. Contrasting behaviors not only occur in the same person, but usually do.

The reason that both sets of symptoms tend to occur in the same person stems from the similarity in adverse learning experiences they had in early childhood. Rebukes about touching genital areas are universal. Sin and Retribution are stamped into the conscience early. We seldom need to tell the child that some things are naughty. He will have learned about most of them from experience at an early age.

The "No!" pronounced by a loving mother brings disappointment to the child. He will avoid evoking disapproval the next time he is in that situation. The act will automatically go into his cognitive storehouse (Freud's unconscious) as sin.

On the other hand, he may develop a defence against rejection by seeking reassurance of his acceptance. The need to peek at breasts may be a child's attempt to learn that everything in the mammary department is alright and functioning. The voyeur's interests in breasts may be rooted in the desire to repeat the comfort found at the mother's breast. On a deeper level we really are dealing with important relationships, not breasts.

Peeking at sexual objects serves the same need as exhibiting them. If you exhibit them then they can be *seen*. Do you see the connection between opposites-- exhibitionists and voyeurs?

For the voyeur, each glimpse of skin, or clothing that covers the body, is a reminder that all is well in the world. This is how sexual fetishes about clothing develop.

The voyeur needs to test limits to make sure he can still get gratification without being punished. Every sexual act he commits successfully reassures him that he can act with impunity. He feels that others will not be punishing him, although persisting guilt reveals that he still is paying a price.

* * * * *

During the last session we became rather maudlin. Jonathan said,

"I've learned more about myself during our sessions than I have about you. I learned enough to see that the liberal standards that you apply for obtaining satisfaction in life are admirable. I even have begun to change my behavior. I am no longer so ready to deny myself the pleasure of an experience just because society views it is immoral or illegal. I find myself wondering what Abraham Murray would do when interesting opportunities arise.

These days I am willing to take more risks and to try new things. I wish we could continue our relationship after you leave the hospital. I know that's not practicable because it would involve needs rooted in our therapeutic relationship, so I will have to settle for just having known you."

GROWN UP

I lacked only two courses to complete my PhD studies when I was sent away for treatment. Faculty and students of Boston University no longer viewed me favourably. Everybody knew of my troubles and they tried to keep their distance from me-- I was on my own. I knew that when I was released I would have to "Get out of Dodge."

My major professor, Dr. Milo Yankowitz was an East European refugee, so he was more tolerant than my American-born committee members. He assured me of his support if I agreed to follow his advice in those difficult times.

He confided that he was going to move to Florida the following year. He offered to take me with him if I wanted to go. He assured me that I would be able to complete my doctoral requirements before we left to establish new lives in Florida. I was in no position to refuse, so I put myself completely in his hands. I felt like I was being driven into exile on some deserted island. At least I had a friend to share my misfortunes and joys.

Dr. Milo was a nice guy, but I knew that he was too good to be true. Even before we left for Florida I learned that I was to be his pimp. He needed me to take the risk of recruiting gay students, who would be ready to enact porno sequences while he watched on the side lines. I understood about perverse sexual needs, so I was ready to assist him.

Only after several weeks of helping him gratify his voyeuristic impulses, did he come out and request my own participation. We were standing together, watching a couple of guys doing each other. I always was stimulated by watching fun-lovers, and that day I couldn't conceal my erection. I didn't resist Milo as he unzipped me and got to work. He was not unattractive and so I submitted to his wishes. It would have been safer to stay out of his games but I was beholden to him.

Our friendship strengthened as we learned how we could share interests. Boston University would grant me the doctorate and I would be in the sunny climes with my dirty little secrets intact. We would travel together to Miami after I completed the degree requirements. I had to get my affairs in order before leaving the Boston area.

Milo became the new Chairman of Social Sciences at Immokalee Tech and I would be his first staff member. I would be appointed Assistant Professor of Anthropology in his new department.

All my months of agonizing about my future had been wasted. All I had needed was to find a kindred spirit, who would help me hide my shit. Now I had a good friend, a respected academic appointment, and a new subculture in which to establish myself. I knew that I would slowly work my way back to becoming the Happy Voyeur.

Before I moved to the Miami area, I had to clean up my messy marriage. My wife and our two-year-old daughter Annie lived in my parents' home while I was locked up. Can you imagine-- a devout Irish Catholic girl with a name like Maureen O'Dowd married to a dedicated sexual pervert like me? Neither could anybody else, but my interests had been more normal when we first married.

I should have stuck to my childhood resolution never to marry. I came to realize that Maureen's needs and mine were too different for us to become synchronized with each other.

During the three years of our marriage I widened my search for extramarital ways to meet my needs. The Catholic Church did not approved of my ideas of fun, even for married couples. At first Maureen thought kinkiness was interesting, but before long, she became obstinate. She refused to play my games and nagged me because I was risking arrest.

When I did get caught, she became antagonistic. She accused me of making our marriage impossible and ruining her life. She never came to my hearings in court or visited me at the hospital. She was wise enough to prefer divorce over spending a miserable life with me.

Thanks to my experiences with Maureen, I decided that I never would remarry. I needed to have pretty girls in my life, but only at a distance. I learned to view my relationships with girls as transactional, a temporary union, beneficial to both.

MIAMI AREA

Narrated by Abraham Murray

JONATHAN P. SLOW

THE GOOD LIFE

I decided to go to Miami for several reasons:

Nobody knew me in Miami.

I liked the outdoor-beachy style of life there.

The people were liberal and tolerant of others.

The Latin American subculture interested me.

To Increase my Spanish language skills.

Warm climate--fewer clothes-- greater voyeur fun.

I threw away my fur jockstrap and packed my swimming trunks with glee. "Florida, here we come!" I was free at last, or at least as free as I could ever be. Can you ever be free as long as needs and impulses determine your destiny?

* * * * *

My girlfriend was a pert 30-year- old when I met her in a Newport nightclub. Bunny was a pole dancer, who gave great lap dances. She was able to accept all the kinky stuff that I came up with. She enjoyed our games but she probably engaged in them more for my pleasure than for her own. But then that's what a voyeur wants in his confederate-- one to perform exciting acts for his benefit. We got along so well that I invited Bunny to come live with me in Miami.

* * * * *

Bunny got mighty lonesome during my last few months in the hospital. She told me about how deprived she was and asked me if it would be alright to bring a man home for a few romps. I realized two things: The need for sexual gratification was going to force her to seek satisfaction. Secondly, she was going to find it whether I agreed or not.

I went along with the inevitable and actually encouraged her. I still wanted to maintain control over her, even if she was making it with another partner. I was able to recognize the likelihood of being displaced by a new stud.

Instead of harassing her, I encouraged her to find a female companion to pass some happy hours with until they released me. She already had engaged in some girly things before she met me.

She smiled sweetly and thanked me, "I'll think about it." She confessed later that she had gone out to a sexy bar that very night and followed my suggestion.

In a bar, she hooked up with an agreeable companion named Kitty. Their friendship grew, and Kitty moved in temporarily with Bunny until I was released. The girls got along so well that they agreed to move to Miami where all of us would live in one residence when Roy and I were released. With a Bunny and a Kitty, I had a whole menagerie of cuddly animals.

We rented a big house in Coral Gables-- that's where the Cuban Americans live. I wanted to be closer to my work and to Miami Beach, but there would be lots of time later to get settled properly. Anyhow, I was eager to familiarize myself with the Hispanic language and culture of Coral Gables. Parts of Coral Gables were so Spanish speaking that you would think that you were in a foreign country. When one of us was going out on an errand, the rest of us would holler, "Don't forget to take your passport!"

Bunny and Kitty were delighted with our new home. They got along famously-- in fact, I was jealous of them. Their relationship lessened my control over both girls. However, Kitty was very sensitive to other's feelings and she set things right by being exceptionally nice to me.

Actually, I'm pretty easy to please. All Kitty had to do to make me happy was to let me sit on a stool while she took a shower with the curtain open. None of us was very jealous so we remained good friends despite some fooling around.

Roy and Kitty became such pals that they married two months after coming to Florida. The marriage was a good thing because it stabilized and marked the family relationships that tend to blur when you occasionally mix it up sexually. We learned to recognize the difference between family loyalty and the lending of body parts to please a friend.

Roy and Kitty's wedding was a festive time; they did it Latin American style. The wild music and dancing excited me so that I lost my head. I was already lubricated with rum so my guard was down. Half-jokingly, I asked, "Bunny, sweetheart, would you marry me? She replied smilingly, "What! And spoil all the sexual fun we have together?" We had a laugh over that and we never spoke of marriage again.

After Roy's marriage, we all became more comfortable and we lived in each other's laps, so to speak. We never closed the bathroom door anymore. When we guys got out of bed with hard-ons, we no longer tried to hide them. The girls went around the house half-clothed when they were in the middle of dressing to go out. The truth is that all of us enjoyed those informal exposures. The girls kept us going until we had a chance to set-up more elaborate and exciting adventures.

Our household was a simplified version of the complete voyeur's playground. Both of us guys had ladies with lovely proportions, and they were delighted to have their bodies worshiped.

Bunny let me see her in all positions and in all activities. I loved watching her in tantalizing play while showering. She never ceased to tease me by lying naked on our bed with a strip of pubic hair showing me the way to delight. Occasionally, Bunny did Kitty the courtesy of inviting her to join us in our couple games.

If Roy or Kitty showed up at the door, we invited them in and improvised. Bunny and I didn't really require others in our games, but it did spice things up considerably. When they joined us, it opened up the opportunity to witness bump and grind scenes that we couldn't attend to when we were busily engaged ourselves.

You probably already think me socially irresponsible, just because I like diversity-- Not so! Roy and I understood the importance of families and about parental responsibility. That's why Roy and I went to a doc-in-the-box when we first arrived in Miami. He clipped our tubes and made us free to splash wherever we wanted without burdening society with accidental fathers.

I bet you're thinking at this point that I wasn't the kind of guy to overlook the chance to enjoy our reflections in mirrors. Of course, we had mirrors on two walls and a larger one on the ceiling. Mirrors make routine sex more exciting for the voyeur.

Voyeurs require distance between them and their subjects. They are not horny bunnies, who just want to get on top as fast as they can. Voyeurs want distance so they can shed their own personality and character, and assume the persona of the target. They prefer the tingling feeling of excitement that comes with naughty spying, more than the gross rush of ejaculation.

* * * * *

Bunny paid her dues in the nightspots of Newport. She learned from her pole-dancing days how to be friendly. She was no whore, but if she liked a guy, she would give him a lap dance he would never forget.

She liked to drag me around Miami Beach, and I had the chance to sit at the table with a lot of exciting stuff. Bunny's associates were the friendly kind, so I got lots of chance to cuddle strange ass. When they came over to our table, I would find myself enveloped in steamy flesh. They smelled of a mixture of sweat and perfume that would seduce a priest.

These blonde entertainers would pop up in the daytime as supporters of entertainment gigs. Bunny and I donated to charity functions quite often. I'm afraid my interest was more sexual than philanthropic. We supported Miss Teenager, Miss Miami Beach, and the Junior Beauty Parade.

I liked the teen-ager contests best. They always needed bachelors to volunteer as judges, and I tried to keep out in front of the crowd so that I would be noticed. I really was just a dirty old man, but we are the guys, who most appreciate such contestants. The girls all reminded me of my daughter Annie. I found it exciting when a girl would put an arm around me and would rub her thighs against me.

Kidding around with a contestant, who reminded me of my daughter, always aroused me. Such incestuous impulses would upset most other men, but I just enjoyed myself all the more. As some dirty old man once said, "Don't knock incest if you haven't tried it."

* * * * *

I agreed to take Bunny to a nude beach. It was a lovely, warm sunshiny afternoon when we arrived. We striped at the entrance and walked hand-in-hand, feeling rather awkward, like everybody else. As we approached the beach, we smiled at passers-bye and tried not to let them see us staring at their bodies. Somehow it seemed inappropriate to have empty hands with all these body parts everywhere. We both needed a cocktail to occupy our hands and keep us out of trouble.

After finishing our drinks, we left the buildings that reminded us of civilization. We padded along the beach down to where unfettered bodily parts were being flung about in a free-for-all volleyball court.

I found myself wishing I were a woman so that my sexual turn-on wouldn't be so noticable. The more I worried about my arousal, the more conspicuous I became. I was ashamed of my condition. I imagined people were staring at me and tittering. I tried to position myself behind Bunny as we arrived at the volleyball court. That didn't work out well because I kept bumping up against her and that just aggravated my problem.

The novelty of nudity started wearing off after watching the players running around for an hour. I started seeing all the fat, flabby flesh as just meat with little or no enticement. That just exposed another worry, What if this experience marks me for life? Will I no longer find flesh exciting, and will I lose my desire for sexual satisfaction? Eventually I recovered from that crude experience and never wanted to try it again. "You can get too much of a good thing!"

* * * * *

The two years after my release were the happiest days of my life, but they couldn't last. The Dade County Court sent Roy away for 20 years. Of course, he told me all about it...

"I was getting ready for bed one night when my 14-year-old niece came in. She sat on my bed and reached over so she could slide her hand up my baggy undershorts. I looked at her in shock, but she smiled and continued exploring. She said, 'Yours won't be the first one I've played with.' My response betrayed both my physical and verbal interest. While she was exploring my erection I was begging her to tell me who else did that with her.

She told me that the bus driver came back to her seat in the school bus after he dropped off all the other kids. He asked her, 'Do you want to play with my nice, friendly dolly?'

I was upset that some scruffy bastard was the one to teach her about sex. I told her, 'It's alright. I won't tell anybody if you don't.' She nodded her head and went back to playing. Of course, the lessons progressed on subsequent nights.

I didn't intend for it to happen but she wanted to try the ultimate action. As I entered her, I thought only of my own selfish pleasure. She startled in pain and tried to pull away. I should have known enough to back off but I didn't.

She left my room in pain; I didn't realize how badly I had hurt her. She went to bed, and woke up in a pool of blood. I knew I was screwed. I had made the biggest mistake of my life.

The police came the next day to cart me away again-- this time for 20 years. I never saw her again."

Kitty found life empty after Roy went away. She was a very dependant sort of person; she had never learned to enjoy her own company. At first, she tried the companionship of a big dog.

One day I went over to her part of the house and I caught her while she was seeking pleasure desperately. She was laying on her back on the floor with her dog jumping around and licking her in interesting places.

She was embarrassed that I caught her in that position, but not so much that she quit. The dog positioned himself so that they both could enjoy the ride. Liberal as she was about sexual matters, she made me promise never to tell anybody about what she had done. I kept my silence until now.

Kitty started searching earnestly for a new male companion, and she found one among the New York vacationers. He was well endowed and had money too, and so she married him. She moved back up north with him, but she continued to visit us every few years. We resurrected the old games, but they weren't as much fun as they used to be-- I missed Roy's company. My circle of deviant friends was narrowing down. Some of my old friends were incarcerated, while still others had tired of partying and spent more time at home.

Kitty, Bunny and I used to make a monthly visit to the prison to see Roy. Kitty told him that she couldn't go on without a life of her own. Roy was reasonable and encouraged her to break with him. She told him about her New York suitor and he seemed happy for her.

We all thought Roy had taken the break-up well, but then we noticed the changes in him. On later visits, he was surly and not very talkative. He was quarrelsome with us and with the prison guards. It was as though he was going around looking for trouble.

He found it in the form of a shiv in the back that ended his worldly concerns. Kitty went to New York soon afterwards.

VOYUERISM

When I was young, I believed that what was forbidden tor children also was forbidden for adults. I couldn't have been more wrong. When I realized that adults had a free pass for sex, I couldn't wait to become a man. I still hoped that my childhood sexual impulses could be controlled and that I would go to Heaven.

All men have a wide variety of things that arouse them sexually or heighten the pleasure of explicit sex. Most men of sensitivity have some preference for particular body parts. Some displace their basic drives with curious affection for fetishes like shoes, braziers, or panties. A perfectly ordinary man may experience shivers of excitement as he inserts his foot into his stocking when dressing for work.

Some men are titty-lovers and others admire asses. Certain public expressions acknowledge the truth about the polymorphic sensuality of men-- "Whatever turns you on," "Whatever scratches your itch," or "Whatever bakes your bread."

* * * * *

The purist voyeur depends upon stimuli to enhance his sexual experience but he tends to avoid physical contact with the actual target. He is a looker, rather than a doer. The purist offers little threat to society because he does not impact it. In reality, there are few purists, so we all end up being classified as "sexual offenders."

* * * * *

The pleasure of graphic arts lies in the portrayal of different aspects of the curved lines and shapes. Straight lines are uninteresting and provide a poor basis for constructing anything except buildings.

You may ask, "Why curves?" You ought to know! You spent the first months of your life cuddling with curvy surfaces. Those rounded milk sacks were the prototypes of all the curves that will smooth the rest of your life.

Life for the infant goes like this:

Imagine that you are only a few weeks old and sitting in Mommy's lap. You have not yet reached the wriggly stage, so your visual field is narrowed to what is in front of you. What do you see? A breast of course! What do you associate with the sight of your mother's breast? Of course, a warmth that runs through your body from hers. The liquid brings peace and comfort. The basic valence of your mother's welcoming nipple has been impressed on you forever. It's your own treasured experience and it will stay with you all your life, although it will reside in the unconscious.

As the infant gets a little older, the more general curves of his mother assail his senses as she holds him in her arms.

He learns that the fleshy folds of her body indicate her nearness, that in turn, gives reassurance that his needs will be met. He is constantly bombard by her round eyes, as she smiles at him from a round, puckered mouth.

He even can chew on the curves of her shoulder, although he prefers the curvature of her breast. Her rounded, soft torso feels good against him. As he looks down he sees rounded thighs, and sometimes the rounded belly that protrudes to make a soft cushion for his head.

We should feel blessed to be surrounded by a soft, rounded world instead of one with sharp useless lines, and furniture with painful corners.

It's no wonder that grown men retain a love of curves and even will break the law to encounter a neighbor's display of them. An acclaimed artist can be satisfied with just sketching nudes in charcoal. Perhaps he is the happy voyeur that we seek to be. He has found an outlet for his urges that is not prohibited by law.

A respectable voyeur values the excitement of stalking a pretty girl more than he would copulating with her, and he avoids actual contact. Most voyeurs are talkers, not doers. They usually are very different in character from the other deviates.

"Confrontation with the victim" is the key to evaluating the danger of deviates. Stalkers are not all alike just because they bear the same label; neither are all exhibitionists the same. The sneaky ones may be annoying but are not dangerous.

The stalker and exhibitionist may be either withdrawn or aggressive. They can be confrontational and dominate the victim through fear. That type depends upon the victim's fear of discovery as a way of avoiding arrest. They also use the victim's guilt over her unconscious desires to welcome the sexual affront. With these sorts, the ultimate confrontation is rape and murder-- the crimes that give us deviates such a bad name.

Most people are repelled by closeness that invades their personal space. Some people become disgusted and impotent when faced with crude genitalia. Confrontation often is an essential part of *frotage,* the sexual act of rubbing the genitals against the victim, that usually occurs in a crowd. Such men dally with confrontation and even toy with public denunciation.

In designating a person as a voyeur, it is important to identify the motivations in his underlying personality. Some are bold and adventurous, and assail society daringly. Others are the timid type, who sneak around in the dark, trembling-- the victims of insecurities and fears. Both are active voyeurs and commit somewhat similar crimes, but they are not the same kind of person on the inside.

The timid soul would like to live more like others and may welcome psychotherapy. He can benefit by changing self-perceptions that can open the door to more acceptable forms of sexual release and conflict reduction. His treatment outcome is rather favourable. The confrontational type person defends himself arrogantly and has little reason to change his behavior.

I confess that I am the Happy Voyeur, not the sad one. I am content with myself; I like myself and my lifestyle. In my case, the prognosis for remediation with therapy is poor and my only motivation for change would be to avoid incarceration.

* * * * *

I abhor giving attention to famous criminals because it encourages them and their imitators. That makes me want to suppress a valuable example of displaced sexuality in a killing monster. Still, I need to use him to drive home my contentions about the potency of displaced sexual urges...

One night in Chicago, a young man stealthily opened a window of a dormitory. He encountered eight student nurses, unprepared and defenceless.

This crime would be of little psychological interest had he just satisfied his carnal lust. Instead, he tied them up and successively tortured each of them to death. His drive was unstoppable.

His psyche was beyond the comprehension of the dozen psychiatrists consulted. Some said that he was psychotic but most agreed that he was sane. The majority were content to label him a Psychopath without a conscience.

Later interviews by psychologists uncovered the clues to understanding his behavior. The perpetrator remained unable to see his actions in perspective. Early family admonitions relating to sin and Hell warped his view of the world so badly that he denied ever masturbating.

One psychologist asked him which was worse, masturbation or killing a person. He chose masturbation. In fact, the forensic evidence pointed to a highly developed sense of morality. He had a conscience but it was distorted and perverted.

He had resisted his urges to relieve himself for many days prior to that night. He couldn't bring himself to masturbate-- it was too sinful. He went out drinking with a friend, and his vague urges led him to wander the streets. He detoured through a dormitory campus area. He had no premeditated plan, no *conscious* intentions.

It just happened. He found himself forcing open a ground floor window and a veil of tingling excitement descended upon his whole body. He developed a painful erection from this excitement, but he persisted.

While penetrating the window to encounter his first three victims, he felt the gush of an involuntary ejaculation. As he climbed into the room, his orgiastic excitement was converting to anger. He was overwhelmed with guilt over his ejaculation. The very existence of these girls was the cause of his seminal desecrations. He was compelled to make them pay for corrupting him. "They weren't fit to live-- no women are!"

He still had a partial erection but his urges had changed. He tried to penetrate a few of the first girls he encountered, but he was too upset to be able to finish. He blamed them for weakening him and he killed them for that.

He proved to the world two things: You should be careful about alienating irrepressible urges from the conscious or they may burst through, uncontrolled and terrible. Secondly, most bizarre and inexplicable acts can be understood with an open-minded, dynamic approach.

* * * * *

Jonathan Slow once wrote about the danger of unbridled, subconscious urges:

"Criminal Sexual Assault is like a hurricane. Its beginnings emerge secretly from the murky depths, of unknown places. The seed is nurtured unwittingly, twisting and turning with unrecognized enmity. It slips out of the shell-case to widen its destructive field.

The rest of the world sleeps on in innocence, but the beast takes form and he begins to growl in anger and frustration. He casts off its tethers as it shakes free, irresistibly surging onward. Where he is headed, no one knows.

Raging and roaring are signs of imminent disaster, but they are ignored and regarded as unimportant. The heated surroundings do nothing to retard its expanding size or to control the fury of the coming disaster.

Inconveniences from the storm are ignored and tolerated. Optimism obscures the truth about the onrushing danger. It will arrive soon and topple even the lowest buildings and it will flood the highest plains.

Then it will be too late to take precautions. The full evil of the event will be described in tomorrow's front-page. Editorials and, letters to the editor will suggest various scapegoats for the negligence behind this national disaster. Fingers will point, and blame will be allocated.

Political action groups will call for emergency meetings and committees will be formed. Politician's will add their spin on the newspaper releases and make budget shifts. They may even add a new director or they may shift funds to create a new department. Nothing they do will reduce future Criminal Sexual Assaults."

* * * * *

I perfected a supra-sexual teaching technique or scenario that surpassed all others. I'm so proud of it that I have to tell you about it.

I had been using hypnosis in my adventurous experiments for some years. People always told me that I had hypnotic eyes, and it must have been true because I used them to advantage. I had the Early Celtic features of dark hair, and the pupils of my eyes were black and penetrating. When I looked at people, most became uncomfortable because they felt as though I were invading their souls.

I had the mysterious quality that the old vaudevillians called, "Animal Magmatism." This was an advantage because it automatically screened out the weak and self-centered people. Those not intimidated by me became loyal friends. So you see I was a natural-born hypnotist.

There were a considerable number of my students, who showed the required suggestibility and an interest in exploring their psyches. I started out with the conventional demonstrations, but that didn't last long. "Give a carpenter a hammer and he'll find a nail to hammer." This voyeur found his tool and hammered away.

Are you seeing the whole picture? Hypnosis gave me the perfect technique to create scenes that voyeurs love to watch. Furthermore, I could prevent the recall of any messy sexual issues that arose. At first I used hypnosis just to help subjects recognize the feelings and attitudes that they had repressed.

Few people can resist wielding the power that maestros possess, and I was no exception. I often violated a trust when a student or friend agreed to undergo hypnosis with me. I used the situation to meet my own needs and interests.

I often made subjects focus on the most secret and repulsive aspects of their sexual lives. Watching them struggle to resist pouring out their souls turned me on. I used hypnotic suggestion of partial amnesia to block out memory for issues arising in hypnosis that subjects found upsetting. Truthfully, I was concerned with obliterating recollections that could prove harmful to me.

Hypnosis is a dangerous tool because it is so powerful. You start innocently making a subject think he is a dog and he will bark like one. Then you realize that you can make a subject believe he is anything, even a sex slave, and he will perform like one.

I found it sexually stimulating to suggest scenes in which subjects imagined that they were engaging in sexual acts. When they experienced orgasm so did I. After cleaning up my clothes, simple hypnotic commands hid all the shit I had evoked. There was no way I could be brought to justice because I never allowed anyone else to witness those sessions.

* * * * *

The last news we received about my psychologist, Jonathan came by mail. A formal-looking envelope arrived one day three years after my release from the hospital. The return address jumped out at me-- it was from Doctor Jonathan P. Slow. I tore the envelope open, delighted with the prospect of our lives becoming entwined once again.

The message was an invitation to the ceremony for the awarding of the PhD in Clinical Psychology to my old friend and therapist. The title of the dissertation appeared at the bottom of the card,

THE PSYCHODYNAMICS OF A MASTER VOYEUR

Bunny and I attended like proud parents. Bunny sat alone because I went off to enjoy the ceremony by lurking in the background and peeping around the corner of the bleachers. There were irresistible sights under those bleachers that I didn't want to miss.

SETTLING IN

The Miami area that I often refer to is an interesting metropolitan area made up of many small communities like Coral Gables. I was familiar with Miami Beach because I wintered there many times with my parents. I became reacquainted with the area during the two years that Roy and I lived in Coral Gables.

Now that Roy was gone it was time to settle down permanently. You may recall that I was hired as Assistant Professor at Immokalee Tech. I had to take my job into consideration in choosing my permanent residence.

Normally you would live close to your work and try to become a part of the community, but not if you are an outsider and the community is Immokalee. I realized that I couldn't survive in such a nondescript community. A short description of the town's background will explain my concerns about making Immokalee my main residence.

It really wasn't a community of people-- it was a "collection" of six thousand individuals. The landowners operated large sugarcane plantations and tomato farms. All the residents were dependent in some way on these large farm operators. Most of the actual rich owners had moved out of the Everglades Swamp and lived elsewhere in landscaped tropical luxury.

A few educated citizens managed to survive alligator attacks, a continuous blanket of mosquitoes, hissing serpents, and drunken Latinos, as well as Native Americans with machetes. All these people wanted a better life for their children.

The *patrones* owned the land and a few politicians to boot, so they demanded that the legislature establish an academic agricultural station in Immokalee. The politicians extended their support because they wanted to engorge governmental bureaucracy by encompassing the academic field.

They wanted to extend control over teachers and support staff so that they could pretend to have friends in respectable positions. Politicians always need friends in high regard to vouch for their incompetent competency. They named the school Immokalee Technical College and a few students wandered onto the campus, much like flies entrapped by a spider.

The fathers felt that their children had as much right to receive a diploma as anybody else's, since they paid such so much money in taxes. The first group to attend classes was made up largely of local farmers' children. Remaining vacancies were filled by unfortunates, who could not get admission to any other institution in the Florida system.

I was grateful for my appointment, so I tried not to make waves. Academic standards were so different from Boston University that I was a little embarrassed by the first graduates.

Population growth over the years amplified social pressures. This small college went from just issuing technical certificates, to offering a two-year Associate of Science degree. All Florida was growing and the community college system couldn't keep up with demand.

The college increased enrolment many times over, and received support to expand the teaching staff. A Social Studies center was added and the search was on for more faculty. Few wanted to work in this hellhole, but the school managed to find an occasional social misfit like me, who wanted to escape from something in the real outside world.

Only the overwhelming number of Spanish-speaking migrant workers were integrated into a group. There were a few blacks, some Seminole Native Americans as well as a sprinkling of Miccosukee brothers. We educators found ourselves struggling to survive in a hostile environment of strange cultures and dangerous pests.

* * * * *

I was spending all my spare time in Coral Gables, in search of a new place to call home. The Florida housing market had just crashed to an unbelievably low degree. Beachfront property was selling for $100,000 and four-bedroom houses on a canal sold for half that price. I bought a Miami Beach condominium with part of my sizeable nest egg from the family fortune.

In addition, I purchased a small two-bedroom house in Immokalee that would meet my needs during the weekdays when I was teaching. It was a two-hour drive between my homes, but the chance to enjoy the fun environment in Miami Beach made it worthwhile

My new home in Miami Beach was large enough to support great parties. A patio surrounded the swimming pool, and an extension of the patio opened off the master bedroom. I couldn't wait to move in and start partying. I intended to attract new weirdos to help me spice up my life.

The new arrangement completed my plan to live in two communities. I put all my eggs in one basket up there in Rhode Island and ended up losing all support.

Miami Beach was in Dade County and Immokalee was in Collier County. Hopefully, notices about any indiscretions committed in one particular county would stay there. Miami was for fun and Immokalee would provide a safe, respectable refuge to fall back on.

Miami Beach was the only place in Florida where you could find liberals. They came down from New York for winter fun. You could party every night if you had the money and the constitution for it. Every week somebody else was testing society's limits.

One New York bachelor named Lewis had a rich attorney for a father. The son could afford to be a regular patron of the bars on the Beach. One night Lewis ran into a bored young lady, who was determined to shake up the world just for the hell of it. Their muddled thinking became clearer after a few cocktails. Lewis asked her to join him in pushing the limits on indecent public behavior.

The law was fairly clear that total nudity in public was forbidden. The courts heard occasional cases involving nudity but that was all old hat by then. Lewis wanted to shock the world by pushing the limits on "lewd behavior."

He invited his partner to engage in sexual intercourse on the padded cushions scattered in the patio around the pool of a nightclub. That proposal in itself was not remarkable, but the invitation to the guests in the bar to come watch was unheard of.

Everybody wondered why somebody hadn't done that before. Everybody, but everybody, trooped out to the patio to watch. These wild and crazy kids did their business without disrobing. Then the manager played his part by calling the police, but not until the couple had finished their business.

The police snapped on the handcuffs and hauled them away. Their supporters made sure that the newspapers knew all about the event. Attorneys showed up at the jail, competing for a chance to hitch up to this publicity generator. It was only the beginning of a six-month-long circus. New York journalists couldn't wait to come down to cover the struggle between innocent naturalists and the Gestapo justice system of Florida.

At the trial, the defence took the position that consensual sex was not lewd behavior or else all of our parents must be engaging in lewd behavior regularly. Statutes prohibiting indecent exposure were not relevant because they had remained dressed.

The judge dismissed the first filing. The proper, legally-minded protectors of our morality were defeated- - they took it personally and persisted legally. They pestered the State Attorney until he consented to charge the couple with Public Indecency.

The defence claimed that no indecency is involved if the spectators consented to the acting out of this interesting scenario. The defence raised the issue that no law placed a limit on the number of observers that would have to be involved for the action to become *"Public* Indecency."* The judge agreed with the defence and dismissed the charges. It became famous as the Lewis' verdict

There was dancing in the Miami Beach streets the night of the latest ruling. The free souls had won a victory. It only remained to be seen how many other liberals would insist on exercising their rights.

They formed small groups to engage in and display intercourse on the Beach. I was right there watching the eternal struggle between expression and suppression. Eventually things settled back to what was normal for the Beach. I was very disappointed because there would be few interesting sexual displays once the revolution subsided.

* * * * *

Years ago I paid $100,000 for my house, now it would bring two million. But I would never sell it because it was indispensable as a babe magnet. It is located within a ten-minute walk of South Beach and its hotels. Whatever fun-lovers were doing, they often dropped by my house, day or night. They knew that if a party wasn't in progress there soon could be.

My guests always felt at home with me. I never insulted my guests by offering them rewards for doing anything kinky. Our fun and play had to be mutually acceptable or it wouldn't happen.

I had several girls, who would stop by, but were not sexually active. I didn't mind because I gained satisfaction from seeing them dressed for the beach, and showing enough skin to be interesting.

One of my girlfriends was a Lesbian named Sally. We enjoyed each other's company and got our loving elsewhere. Sometimes Sally's girlfriend accompanied her. If I got lucky, the fooling around got raunchy and I got to see the Lesbians going at it from close up.

People automatically assume that Lesbians can't enjoy some sexual kidding around with a guy-- they are wrong. Sally and I had a game that we enjoyed playing together. It took just a little planning-- she had to have stowed her panties somewhere…

After exchanging news, I invite Sally to have some biscuits with tea. She always agrees and shows it with a broad anticipatory smile. She stalls with small talk and we are both tense with anticipation. I start twitching down below.

Sally rises slowly, goes to the kitchen countertop, and kneels on it. Her skirt hitches up to reveal her calves and the lower part of her thighs. She stretches slowly to reach the very top shelf to grab a biscuit. As she does so, her skirt rises up over her hips and she shows all. I grasp myself in ecstasy and tell her to take her time at finding something she likes. She does and I do, and then she slowly descends and smiles as she looks at my wasted manhood.

She never feels threatened because she knows that I won't force sex on her. That's the secret of my beach boy success-- meet the partner's needs but don't push.

Sally was a party girl, so she had many contacts. Sometimes she showed up with a friend or two in tow. She had friends of both sexes, and I often didn't know their preferences. They were all guests in my house and I wanted them to feel free from any pressure. From the days of British colonialism... "Softly, softly catchee monkey." Sometimes I got to see a guest couple make love. As usual, I got my kicks more from watching than in actually participating.

My house on the beach was not my only babe-magnet. I bought a 28-ft. cabin cruiser with two inboard engines. I wasn't a fisherman, so I couldn't justify such an expensive boat unless it proved useful. When I bought the boat I didn't realize that boats were a necessity not a luxury. You had to own a boat if you wanted to live the beach life.

It didn't matter much what you did with the boat so long as it involved entrapping young flesh in the small cabin area. Chicks entered my trap eagerly, and sometimes worked their way out by being compliant. Pickups from the beach usually were too rigid to be able to appreciate alternative means of achieving sexual satisfaction. They understood intercourse but not much else.

Girl guests on my boat only had to show me some of their corporeal charms and I would release them to seek out gratification elsewhere. I was not a stud available to any and all. I was neither rigid, nor a pig, and I was seldom desperate. I knew that there were more pebbles on the beach.

My boat offered me the protection of isolation from cops assigned to entrap the public with wiretaps and recorders. Girls were ready to do things behind the veil of maritime isolation that they would not risk doing in land-based quarters. My boat was a floating pleasure palace and the girls realized it.

The one shortcoming of playing around in the cruiser was the closeness introduced by the cabin size. Even if I only wanted a friendly conversation, I still found myself dumped into the arms of my partner in the adjacent bunk. I was forced to accept close physical contact, whereas my preference was for distant excitement.

Actually, the boat served two purposes. Besides being a girl-magnet, it was a spy outpost. It provided the protection that permitted me to observe people's hidden quirks. I could sneak up a little way from the shore and anchor in a beach area. The small spray-washed portholes let me watch the sunbathers and the loungers in partial disarray. I could view a dozen cleavages with a slight twist of the neck and there was no risk of being seen, unless someone clambered aboard.

In my boat I could be alone with no one to observe or censor me. I could undress as I wished and I could caress myself as the urge bade me. There was nobody to interfere with my voyeuristic elaborations, and I was free to slip into uninterrupted sexual fantasies.

These elaborate sexual fantasies that come with voyeurism require complete abandonment. You don't want to have to worry about somebody knocking on your door. With a boat, nobody can walk up close enough to see in your windows because water surrounds you, not concrete. Girls like the isolation of a boat-- they feel liberated and protected from the world. When you get lucky they tear off their clothes...

I used to anchor in shallow water close to the edge of the shore. Almost any target would do. I would concentrate on one person on the beach-- maybe a plain, ordinary woman. She immediately takes on beauty and other gentle qualities.

My new partner reaches out her arms to give me a luxurious embrace. Her breasts enfold me. She assures me of fulfilment while arousing the fires of passion in me. When it is over there are no regretful partners or complaints.

Voyeurs live to gratify their needs with fantasies. In my cabin, my unfettered mind spots two strangers, relaxing side-by-side on the beach. My imagination animates them:

He slithers over to share her cushion. I almost see the acceptance in her eyes. His bulge speaks for him. Before long, my eager mind forces them to embrace. Their desperate clutching and struggling brings them closer together until they are united. That fulfils my dream. I don't require completion.

No, I couldn't give up my boat.

THE PROFSSOR

Sex started getting boring after living and playing on the Beach for a few years. Even voyeurism was beginning to lose its fascination. It was then that I drifted into teaching voyeurism so that others could exploit their natural sexual capacities more fully.

I accepted only appealing young men as students. Women can learn to enrich their lovemaking by improving foreplay, but they don't make good voyeurs. They don't have the kinkiness in their souls required to become really good voyeurs.

There's nothing wrong with spying on virile guys, it's just not my cup of tea. Our futures just lay along different paths

Some men are better prospects than others are. An adequate level of social maturity is essential in a student. I look for the rare combination of narcissism with sensitivity.

The student must be committed, just like a priest entering a monastery. Both novices have to be ready to disengage themselves from their materialistic, narcissistic focus, and be able to let their spirit enter into the body of another. The gratifications of voyeurism only can be obtained fully by transmuting your own body into another's. Fulfilment of Supreme Bliss is possible only when you have become that other person.

139

Your own physical responses become mere echoes of the other person's feelings.

Transcendentalism is the underlying basis for all of my training exercises. You will recognize the similarity to some of the principles of Yoga, and there are strong elements of hypnosis in these procedures as well.

The whole curriculum is based on the "Three-stage" training process. The focus is on "Being" not on "Experiencing." A master voyeur is a transmigrator of souls, not just a clumsy Peeping Tom. My training process is known to only a few:

The student sits naked in a chair facing the master, who sits opposite. Their bodies are about three feet apart. There must be no external, visual or auditory distraction during the practice session. The exercises are best conducted after dark, and the room should be sealed so that no one can bother them.

The student closes his eyes and attends to the master's soft, comforting voice. The student spends the first ten-minute period identifying and reporting his bodily sensations. He focuses his attention on his circulatory system as well as the tactile sensations from the pressure of his body against the chair. He will feel the gravitational tug on the body parts attached to his torso. He eventually develops an erection but he is not allowed to touch his body.

During the second stage, his bodily sensations become more expansive. He is encouraged to think of his body as a whole. Sensations, once separate are merged in his perception. He feels like he is floating around in the warm clouds of comfort that surround him.

The demarcation between his body and the rest of the world slips away slowly. He seems to be losing his grasp of the world. The space separating him from the master becomes a dimensionless cloud and they merge toward each other.

His erection intensifies somewhat, but he is only aware of the warm comfort that flows throughout his whole body. The warmth of the ambience merges with him. He is no longer a separate being. Only sketchy demarcations of self seem familiar as he becomes part of the world. He relaxes even more completely so that he can enjoy this experience fully.

The warmth that was located in the groin spreads slowly over the rest of him. This heat flows out to the master and envelops them both. They are drowning in an overflow of feelings, and he realizes that this was meant to be.

This is the stage when suggestions are made to produce stimulating sexual imagery.

The student will see draped forms drift teasingly in and out of the foggy mist. Occasional, nipple or vagina-like images emerge to coax him on to the exciting conclusion of the third stage. The mind's eye floats along exciting curves to envelop these sexual parts. Deep, rarely experienced feelings are supported by the general sense of well-being.

As the student moves along in the third stage, the maestro induces visions of men and women engaging in slow, stimulating foreplay. Mouth and lips are drooling and they evoke the subject's own passion. Gentle hands are everywhere grasping, pulling, and caressing. He sees couples engaged in intercourse as though he is astride a motion-picture camera, scanning in panorama mode.

The third ten-minute stage is nothing more than a continuation of the earlier stages. The transmigration of soul continues and the student observes dimly that he is no longer in control of his body. It even seems as though his body is completely detached, and in the hands of the master.

As the process continues, the student shakes free from his dried cocoon body, leaving it behind in the chair. Simultaneously, he slides into the teacher's body. Then the juices of this great throbbing mass of sensation flow together.

As the student returns to the world of reality, he is surprized to find that he had a seminal emission without even touching himself. That conclusion is the reward for the student's dedication.

PRACTICUM

We covered the use of magazines and disks as targets for meeting a student's needs. There was little to discuss about ready-made pornography vehicles-- you just go to the store and buy what turns you on. Home videos and the production of commercial pornography get into a whole different area.

Some of my students were interested in pursuing a career producing artistic or pornographic items. I referred them to the performing arts programs available in the Miami area. They might start out as voyeurs, and make a good living while indulging in their naughty urges. Perhaps some would become rich producers of pornography.

The safest, easiest route to satisfaction is to lock yourself in a bathroom with a copy of Playboy, but we are not adolescents focussed on physical gratification. These pre-recorded targets offer zero risk of getting you caught in the act. Choosing safe targets eliminates risk, but also leaves you without the thrill of the chase. Looking at these safe targets is like eating toast without butter, or potato without salt. Voyeurs require spice with their meals.

We all like to get away with something that we shouldn't do. Voyeurs are seduced by the excitement of avoiding capture. This can be carried too far, and you may encounter serious consequences that take the fun out of breaking the law. Messing with little girls is one such spider web waiting to ensnare some of us.

It has become standard practice for vice officers to sit on their asses and search the internet for evidence that might lead to an indictable offense. Be careful, who you talk to. Seductive flirtation on the net with minors, or sending them a "nudie," can bring a long jail sentence.

You are risking as much as 20 years in jail if you have child porno pictures on your computer. Get rid of them! Plant them on somebody you don't like-- maybe a boss.

The police slink around trying to tempt us to stray off the straight path. They arrange the rendezvous and arrest the poor victim. He was provoked into carrying out a meeting with a Judas Goat, but that is not the same as committing a sex crime. Jail time will be the same even though the police initiated the first step.

* * * * *

Once the classroom lessons were finished, we moved on to the practical side of Voyeurism-- peeping and not getting caught. It was time to spy on real people in the outside world. We reviewed positioning, risk assessment, handling interrogation, and use of alibis and excuses.

In the practicum you learn that voyeurism is hard work, and that planning a project takes considerable patience. Elaborate surveillance excursions are not simple affairs. You have to plan well to reduce risk so that you will be able to continue to enjoy your life.

You don't have to engage in reckless expeditions. Just organizing a special job can keep you occupied with smaller satisfactions Most of the preparation time will be spent lounging at the pool of the apartment complex with a towel covering your crotch.

Meanderings along the city streets can provide bread and butter sustenance for the Voyeur. Freaks and oddballs that he encounters are an interesting change from the usual voluptuous sexual targets. They remind you that plain old innocent gawking can be entertaining.

* * * * *

We begin the practicum with a single, live target. I have the student prepare a plan to spy into my own house, to catch me engaged in private, embarrassing situations:

First they have to establish where the bedroom and bath windows are located. Those are the places where body exposure is most likely to be encountered. Next, they evaluate the degree of risk for each of the two possible windows.

Is there any shrubbery near either window? Are the bushes higher in one location than the other? Does one of the windows open onto the street? Is there an alley alongside the house that might aid escape? Does escape from either window area entail rough terrain that might lead to you being tripped in case of pursuit?

Is one window closer to your exit route from the complex like a street busy with pedestrians or a parked car? Has the mailman completed his rounds? Is there a daytime guard on duty? How about night-time?

Do you have your phoney identification in your pocket? Bogus documents may not stand close scrutiny, but can introduce a delay in calling the authorities. During that short delay, the apprehender might develop doubts and decide not to report his suspicions. Does your false identity provide you with a plausible reason to be on the grounds?

It doesn't hurt to look good to the police if they have detained you on the scene. The jury is out as to the benefit of having a Policeperson's Benevolent Association courtesy card in your wallet. The card shows that you made a donation to their fund and entitles you to courtesy and nothing more. It probably is a worthwhile investment in high exposure activities like voyeurism. You want to impress the police favourably, so keep your record clean by paying all your traffic tickets promptly.

My student must make a final assessment of probable success, and the associated final degree of risk. If the lesson is well thought through, then we put the plan into action---

I wait at home, and go about my usual indoor activities as if it were a normal day. The student arrives by bicycle, car, or on foot-- however the plan specifies. I watch TV and go to bed at my usual time, following the usual routine of bedtime tasks.

We meet the next day to compare notes. The result is a simple pass or fail based upon outcome. If the student can tell me the color of my underwear then it's a pass.

If I have to clear him with an apprehender or if he fails to learn the correct color, then it's a clear fail. I don't take any payment for my instruction-- I'm content with the vicarious benefits of the job. As you would suppose, I'm not likely to keep a student, who fails these practicum tests.

* * * * *

The Police Academy in Washington produces sets of tapes simulating interrogations of a variety of suspects for different offenses. I selected a few from the ones related to first-class misdemeanors and third-class felonies. A spare room in my house served as an interrogation room. Both the student and I had remote controllers to access stopping points on the tape that merit discussion.

The rules for surviving interrogation are as follows:

Reveal little or nothing to the interrogator, but at the same time appear to be cooperative. It's important to remember that once you are apprehended your main concern should be to get the charges dropped.

The second thing to remember is that every policeperson is your adversary in such a contest. There are no friendly policepersons-- they are just people doing their job. They will smile at you while they are lying. Friendly remarks don't mean that they like you. *They want to put you away for as long as possible!*

You must constantly remind yourself that you are no longer a child following a blind moral code to make your parents happy with you. You have been detained as a suspect, so you will have to lie. There is nothing much an examiner can do even if he knows that you are lying.

If you are guilty, then everybody expects you to lie. Lying in self-defence is legal and entails no consequences. They will be trying to get you into the "guilty mode" by chiding you for lying. If they can make you feel guilty over lying, then they are on their way to making you feel that you are a naughty tot that deserves to be punished. If they can make you feel guilty over minor matters, then confession will follow closely.

You can start out with the big lie-- "I didn't do it!" Then fabricate a believable story and stick to it. Avoid overloading your version with too many details or you will forget what you said and contradict yourself in the retelling. Keep your lie as close to the truth as possible so that during re-examination you will be able to repeat it.

A coordinated team will be examining you most of the time. The police almost automatically slip into the Good Cop-Bad Cop roles. Why do you think two examiners are in the room? Maybe you think the police don't have enough work to do so the team up to hang out together. Perhaps, it takes two of them to come up with twice as many questions. No, it's because they can't play their game just using one good cop or one bad cop.

You have to remember that the police have slipped into pre-arranged roles from the time you were physically encountered. Their role-playing is the most important aspect of managing a suspect in custody.

It may look like they are interacting with you in a genuine, open manner; but they never are. They have conducted so many interviews that their responses are automatic. The show must go on!

149

The bad cop will pretend that he is shocked that a citizen like you would engage in such criminal action. He is merely prodding your conscience. Actually, he couldn't care less about your misdemeanor offense. His big concern is to stay alive and to keep the citizens from killing one another. Dealing with petty crime is just so much bullshit.

You will be upset when apprehended. You will be in no condition to make wise decisions about what to say to the police. Be firm in requiring that your lawyer be present during questioning.

It is standard routine for the police to push for a quick solution. They are lazy and too busy to dig out the case information, so they want you to supply it. They will pretend that you can have all the time in the world to realize the seriousness of your situation. The stewing period is part of most interrogations.

Do not consider accepting any offers of special treatment that you must respond to immediately. Offers to cut a deal are made from weak positions. If they encourage you to accept a deal then you can take comfort in knowing that their evidence is weak at that point. Cool but not arrogant, is the way to go.

Remember that the police want to close cases as conveniently as possible. Don't assist them by making a confession or ratting out a confederate. Never give up your advantage without your attorney's approval. Make them earn their doughnuts!

CAVEATS

You must be wary when you're drinking with friends. Be careful not to take your own criminal sexual exploits too lightly. Bar mates will be interested in your stories of encounters and you will enjoy being in the limelight. Revealed secrets can reach the wrong ears and you may find yourself staring into the glaring light of an interrogation room. Avoid the indulgence of bragging to your friends.

The safest way to commit a sex crime is to work alone. Avoid inviting others to share in your criminal act; they can become witnesses against you. If you must use a confederate, then make sure he is at as much risk as you are. If a professional takes on an amateur partner then he greatly increases his danger.

If you are caught, it's comforting to have a partner to help share the blame and to commiserate with you, but there is a serious downside. Having a partner, who was caught at the scene, increases your risk too much. You can't control the information he gives the police-- he can rat you out.

If you have a partner, the police keep you separated after arrest so that you can't control the flow of information. This precaution permits the police to turn partners against one another. You can spoil their game by never giving them any information without getting the advice of your attorney.

* * * * *

Blind alleys and dead-end streets present both advantages and disadvantages to the voyeur. Both locations have fewer potential witnesses, so you can obtain your objective with less risk of being caught. On the other hand, if you are found in an alley or a dead-end street it's harder to come up with an excuse for being there.

This quandary is similar to the one as to whether to peek during the daylight hours or at night. You are safer at night because fewer people are about and you are less likely to be seen. On the other hand, if you are caught, it's hard to explain why you are trespassing after normal hours. The final decision may depend upon traffic density. If a large number of people are moving about during the day, you may be forced to make your approach in the most secluded area or at night-time.

Disguise your intentions by what you carry when you go for a walk. A medium-sized sack of groceries may be helpful. In fact, it can be useful to have a store nearby that you might be coming from. True, a clerk won't remember your purchases, but you would be using the store only as a bluff to discourage anybody from detaining you further.

It can be very embarrassing if you are caught in the act of peeking in a window with your fly open. It gets worse when the witness says in court that, "The accused had an erection." The students needed to learn how to make that evidence disappear quickly.

Nurses developed the "Brute Killer Maneuver" to do just that. When an erection gets in the way of nursing care, they place the left palm under the shaft and sharply slap the top of the shaft with the right palm.

With a sharp slap of the wrist, it will be soft and non-incriminating by the time anybody gets close enough to apprehend you. Note especially to nurses: Overuse of this deterrent can cause lasting impotence. Perhaps regular slapping by nurses should become part of the treatment regime for all detained sex offenders!

Don't worry too much if there isn't time enough to zip up your fly. There is no law against having an unzipped fly unless something is projecting from it. Court rulings have established that pieces of clothing do not qualify as being "Lewd or Indecent." Nonetheless, I've seen some pretty hot beach wraps that could have turned those judges on.

Never carry a knife, not even a pocket-sized jack-knife. The D.A. will be looking for ways to elevate the seriousness of your little romp. He will argue that carrying a weapon shows premeditation and makes the case more serious. The D.A. is your antagonist, he wants to convict you and get the longest sentence possible. He is always on the watch for ways to strengthen his brag-sheet about his cases.

You need a residence of your own, so you might as well settle for one that meets both daily needs and voyeuristic ones. Neighborhoods, composed of houses, have spreading lawns. Generally, open spaces just mean you will be easier to see and follow in a chase. Condos are a better choice.

Do have a dog. Wherever I lived I had a dog that needed to be walked every evening about the time that some people forget to draw their curtains. Dogs are indispensable for the voyeur; they provide an even better cover story than, "I just couldn't hold it until I got home!" You can blame the dog for dragging you into the bushes alongside the window.

A bitch that is large enough to withstand sexual assault by neighborhood dogs serves another purpose. When she's in heat you tie her out in the yard like a Judas Goat. Then you stretch out in your lounge chair and wait for her scent to drift around the complex. A prowling stud will come along eventually.

If you're lucky, there will be two or more dogs ready to fight for the right to mount her. If there is only one, she may be reluctant to submit. Natural Selection has fashioned her to make an active choice from a pack of eager pursuers. That way the bloodline will be kept strong through puppies from the healthy victor's genes.

They will fight for the bitch and may even kill a competitor. You should never intervene to separate them because they might turn on you. They might think you want the bitch too.

For once you will be on high moral ground. You can just sit back and enjoy the show. "My dog and I were sitting in our yard and those brutes were allowed to run loose. They came over and assaulted my dog without provocation."

Eventually, one stud will win out and clasp his prize. Their copulating is not terribly arousing but at least it still is legal for animals to engage in sexual acts in public.

Often the excitement of the contest is more interesting to watch than the culmination. Once in a while you get a special laugh when the stud is stuck in the bitch by the swelling of his blood-engorged penis. The antics they can go through to disengage are hilarious enough to overshadow the sexual aspects.

* * * * *

School playgrounds are very inviting. You can pull up close to the subjects and cover your busy hands with a coat. Best of all you get to see lots of cute kids.

The immediate problem with viewing children is that the adults responsible for the children's safety are vigilant. They know that schoolyards are magnets for molesters. The big problem is that judges and juries use large sentencing multipliers if the perp uses force or the action involves children.

You don't want to antagonize the whole community, so it's best to beat feet if you come across children under 16 years-of-age. Always avoid the natural temptation to sit little girls on your lap or pat their bottoms, even if they are family.

There are several advantages to viewing from a car instead of standing outside a condo. First, you are scrunched down, so you will be less likely to be noticed. Also, witnesses have less time to study your face if you are on the move. You can drive away slowly if adults show signs of suspecting your intentions. If openly accosted then you can escape quickly.

The high seating of trucks almost completely hides your lap area in the cab, but lets you look out in front of you. Often, trucks bear identifying characteristics that make them easy to trace back to you. Campers are a much better choice because your visual fields to the sides and rear are not so restricted, as with a truck.

The big problem of using a car or truck for your games is that it ties you to it. You may escape the scene by vehicle, but someone may have written down the license plate number. Traces of tread marks in the parking area can provide the evidence that leads to your conviction.

Actually, my preferred approach to a target is by bicycle. The bike is not easily identified and yet it provides rapid escape. The disadvantage to the bike is that you are so exposed that everyone can see what you are up to.

Don't get casual about your excursions, even though they resemble "A walk in the park." In other words, plan your event and leave nothing to chance. Know when a guard is on duty and what his route is. You can walk the area safely by staying on the sidewalks or by using the roadways. If you are seen up on a lawn you might alert a resident. Above all, choose your targets carefully. Don't just select an unknown target because it looks interesting. Make your selection on the basis of what you learned on previous scouting trips.

Never leave behind traces of yourself at the scene. Keep your hands free of encumbrances that you might forget or that could hamper your escape. Don't toss out food wrappers or cigarette butts. Never ever leave behind you a little puddle of your DNA for the cops to analyse-- always use a condom and take it away with you when you leave. Never take anything from the premises; don't keep telltale souvenirs of your victories.

Have you ever felt that you were being followed as you walked along on the street? It probably wouldn't occur to you that a stranger was busy with something besides walking. You may have made his day without ever knowing about it.

Wearing a condom makes it easy to enjoy a voyeuristic walk in a public area. You can cut out a side pocket of some old pants or wear a raincoat to disguise your evil designs.

Generally, I prefer the on-foot approach for studying my targets. The main weakness to that approach is that you usually have to settle for passing glimpses of your moving target.

Venues suitable for this stalking can be sidewalks or even interiors of buildings. I especially like libraries. Your grasp on a book in one hand shows your ostensive reason for being there. You can hide your other hand in your clothing. With your other hand in the pocket, you appear to be just another visitor engaged in literary pursuits.

Proper apparel can help you mollify the rage of an angry resident. Always dress modestly but neatly. Dress up or down to fit in with the class of people in your target area.

Are you going to wear a uniform to identify you as some sort of worker called into the area to correct a problem? Most of the time I make my residential excursions in a maintenance uniform. I use a generic one that has a manufacturer's patch on the front and the word "maintenance" across the shoulders.

* * * * *

Once in a while I go on an expedition to a movie house. I hang around outside until an attractive lone woman buys a ticket. I follow her and sit alongside her with an empty seat separating us. I never alarm her by saying hello or smiling.

I watch her while she watches the movie. If she catches on and calls the usher then I'm off like a flash. I suspect that some of the times I have enjoyed this game the women knew what I was up to. They were passive accomplices in carrying out my naughty game. Some may have been sure that I was a dangerous predator and were too frightened to complain. A few would be too embarrassed to create a fuss and a rare one might have admitted that she enjoyed the attention.

Even women can be a bit perverted too, as was confirmed during one of my visits to a movie theatre:

> When I turned to look at my target I found her staring at me. After a few minutes she smiled at me but said nothing. A few minutes later she beckoned to me. I nonchalantly slid over into the seat next to her.

> After a few minutes she unzipped me. I tried to remain cool but she took my hand and pushed it up under her dress. She wasn't wearing panties so I knew that she was my kind of person. Neither of us spoke a single word, not even to say goodbye. It just proved the old saying that: You don't have to talk a lot to have fun."

SEXUAL PREFERENCE

Homosexuality is still practiced the same old way, but what the word signifies has changed during the past century. At first it was a label for a type of immoral criminal predator. After the turn of the century, the medical quacks moved in and pushed aside the preachers and the jailors. They declared that homosexuality was a type of medical pathology, a disease. They gave it the label, Sexual Psychopath.

Homosexuality used to be a "Sexually Handicapped" disorder (for making children). Now it is socially acceptable, even laudable to show this flexibility in adopting a lifestyle. Homosexuality is not only sanctioned by law, but is rewarded with financial benefits for joining your life with a same-sex mate.

Voyeurism requires bodily appreciation but does not erect sharp limits based upon gender. You may wonder about my own sexual orientation. Like most voyeurs, my focus is on pleasure and satisfaction. All of us voyeurs are social outcasts, so it matters little if we are reviled also for having homosexual tendencies.

The origins of voyeurism may be the mother's soft curves, but that doesn't mean we can't appreciate the *lingam* statues of phalluses so common in primitive societies. Peak experiences in sex and artistic expression, combine in any culture to give the greatest joy.

The voyeur should not be forced to choose between anatomical parts that embrace and those that protrude. No. All of us should appreciate the sources of joy that God has granted us. I always have admired the directness of studs, who would fuck anything: They go up to the hole in the barrel and plunge in. The next day it's their turn in the barrel, but it's all fun.

Certainly, the phallus is an exciting and attractive art form, but the soft, curving breast is equally attractive. A primitive instinctual need grasps males to divert them from a selfish penis focus, to embrace the mother image, *Pacha Mama*. But the voyeur is too devious just to go search for the contentment found in cuddling with a woman's body.

I have the capacity to engage in homosexual activities and can become excited while watching two guys making out. I'm not very good at working up enthusiasm just from viewing guys in the locker room.

The urine-pheromone smell of public toilets is disgusting for most people, but it has a certain appeal for us, who are into kinky in a big way. The genital smell awakens hopes and dreams of rewarding sexual contacts.

It's easier to find gays willing to play toilet games than to locate female sexual playmates. Men are animals, ever ready to ejaculate however and wherever they may be. They congregate around urinals, longing for a gratifying encounter, and sometimes I join them.

Women require at least a pretense of romance and the possibility of making a nest.

I accept these encounters for what they are-- fun that will suffice until I find a more interesting heterosexual one. I don't even care all that much who does what to whom. I love any kind of sex! You might call me a flexible voyeur because one day it's AC and the next DC. I return to focus on the female form, like any other true voyeur.

To answer your question, I only train young males to become successful voyeurs. Their focus and that of the program is heterosexual, but who doesn't like a little divergent fun on the side?

Women don't make very good voyeurs because they are nest-makers. They view corporeal conjoining as a means to an end. They view the animal-side of making love as an unfortunate accompaniment. Most women pretend to enjoy sex because it is a good way to lead their significant other around by the balls.

Actually, I like gays as friends more than I do Lesbians. It's true that Lesbians can bring more flies into my trap, but I'm not very good at dealing with women's complicated feelings of romance. Sex is fun in all forms and everybody should enjoy it.

LEGALITIES

One incident involved a neighbor on the right side of my property. She complained to her friends about me because I was spying on my neighbor on the left. My neighbor on the left and I had an unspoken, mutual understanding. She had been married for 20 years and desperately needed a younger man to show a reassuring interest in her physically.

It started one day while I was visiting her-- she accused me coquettishly of peeking in at her window. I told her jokingly that I couldn't resist the desire to see more of her charms. She giggled and said, "Well, I guess it doesn't do any harm to let you have a little peek once in a while." When she saw me outdoors after our talk, she drew her bedroom blinds wide open as well as well the front of her dressing gown.

After a month the neighbor on the right caught on to what we were up to. She couldn't stand to see her neighbor being appreciated. She consulted her minister and he advised her to file a formal complaint with the police.

She hadn't thought through the consequences of such action. My attorney tried to help her realize that she would be the laughing stock of the community if she pursued this petty complaint. Like other narrow-minded people, she persisted until I found myself being interrogated.

That whole process was never placed in my record, because the prosecutor couldn't find any law that I had broken. There is no law prohibiting consensual voyeurism and they weren't about to charge me with Operating a Public Nuisance. Maybe everybody involved learned a lesson-- "Everything kinky doesn't have to be illegal."

That little fiasco encouraged contentious others to ask the Dade County courts to set stricter limits. The Baptists wanted all nudity to be regarded as instances of lewd behavior. Liberals, like me, wanted legislation to guarantee the people the right to do with their bodies as they wished, as long as they did it in private or with consenting adults.

The battles went on in the courts for the next 20 years. Some of it even overflowed into the streets, as was bound to occur with an excitable Hispanic population. Citizens with strong moral standards, hot-tempers, and sharp machetes tried to settle the issues that the courts couldn't.

The issues related to sexual misbehavior became even more muddled over time. The courts were bombarded by auxiliary questions-- Is showing cleavage to be exempted? Would showing more than half the breast be excessive and therefore, indictable? How long must a skirt be to avoid being obscene? Would girls in bikinis have to wear towels when not in the water?

Was it lawful for a man to watch several nude women at a time? If he did observe a group of nude girls on a beach, should he be charged with multiple infractions? What if he watched the same girl for several days in succession, would that lead to multiple charges? What if the girl was his wife?

Liberals realized that passing restrictive laws about exposure constituted attacks on their human rights. It seemed like there was a conspiracy to deprive them of their sexual and marital rights.

Would new laws require that the bedroom light be extinguished when husband and wife copulate? Would the wife have to be sure that none of the family was watching when she slipped slinky lingerie over her enticing form? Would she have to exclude the husband from her dressing room?

Will fathers still be allowed to put their little girls to bed? Would it be against the law to pat their fannies when saying goodnight? Would the legislation prohibit a man from bathing his daughter if she is older than two? Should he be excluded from the room when the mother is dressing their daughter?

Once you get all those questions sorted out, the controversy can start all over again. Would the statutes against voyeurism be specifically for female targets or would they apply equally to men looking at men?

What about people, who get a thrill by looking down at themselves, should they be arrested too? What if you admire yourself in the mirror, would you have to cover your delicate parts?

If you look at Playboy illustrations are you guilty of violating voyeuristic prohibitions? Would the penalties be of the same severity if video disks were used instead of still magazine pictures? Should a farmer be punished for lifting the tail of his sheep in order to shear her?

If a woman lounges nude in her fenced yard, is that OK? If the yard is unfenced but surrounded by wilderness, how far away from public access should it be? If she can be seen with binoculars from a public access road, how great a distance should separate them? What lens magnification for binoculars would be acceptable in supporting a charge of lewdness?

If I send a nudie to my girlfriend, would it violate some law? Probably not, unless I went public. What if I send it to three girlfriends, is that going public? How about 1000?

What if Playboy illustrations are merely seductive nudes drawn by the artist, Petty and not photographs of people at all? Do you break the law when you look at drawings of nudes? What about photos of nude drawings? Are career artists breaking the law all their lives? Aren't they voyeurs? Shouldn't they be punished just like us?

Then, the time of day the alleged crime was committed might be considered. Should a night-time crime be punished more severely because it occurred during ominous hours?

If you are a Seminole on the reservation then your every-day behavior can't be restricted by Federal justice regulations, only by tribal law. The Feds can't stop a Seminole woman on a reservation from showing her titties, ass, and everything. Maybe I should try to claim Native American heritage. They get to live in the semi-nude, pay no taxes and have a generous monthly stipend payment, all without raising a finger.

What special circumstances should be taken into consideration when determining sentences? If the target is married, should the penalty be more severe because her whole family was insulted? Should longer sentences be given when the plaintiffs are Baptists, because they would be more upset? What about Catholics? Should the court lengthen the sentence if Muslim members of the community are the complainants because they would be the most outraged?

SNEAKING AROUND

Voyeurs want to know everybody else's secrets but try to hide their own. Apartment complexes have transparent walls. Every night someone in the heat of passion forgets to pull down a shade. The chances of getting exciting glimpses are pretty good in apartment housing. Unfortunately, the chance of getting caught are also high because so many people are scurrying about.

The same human goodies are on display in condo clusters but the units are better separated than apartments. Condo owners know less about their neighbors than do the sardine-packed residents in apartments. Chances are that you can wander about the condo housing units longer without being detained.

Isolated, stand-alone houses are perfect for spying except that you have one hell of a time coming up with an excuse for standing beneath somebody else's window, "Oh! I was just going to the store to buy some milk for my coffee," doesn't work very well.

You must keep a guard dog no matter what kind of residence you have. He will discourage thieves from coming into your yard, and he will intimidate any resident, who catches you in his yard.

You need a large enough dog to make your story credible when you say, "He's so big that he drags me along everywhere he goes." If you stick to your story about walking your dog, a resident is less likely to grab you by the collar to hold you for the police. If the dog growls, so much the better-- the neighbor will be in less of a hurry to call you a liar. The snarling and tugging at the leash restores peace to the neighbourhood more quickly.

You might want to take lots of children with you. The confusion will obscure what you are up to. Use the children on walks just as you do the dog. If neighbors stop you, you just explain that your wife wanted you to take the kids for a walk. If a kid speaks up to spoil your alibi, you can always cuff him alongside the head and declare, "You know how kids are!"

The chief trouble with using kids on an outing is explaining to them, why your hand is jumping around in your pocket. I guess you should have kids too young to know what you're up to, or else old enough to join in the games. If they're just old enough to be curious, you can always try, "I've got a bird with a broken wing that keeps trying to get out of my pocket." Good luck with that one!

* * * * *

Potency and its ugly sister impotence, play a big part in the lives of all men, but especially for the voyeur. Before examining the roots of impotence, it will be helpful to review the physiological aspects of potency. Then we can examine how early learning experiences lead to the unfortunate condition called impotence or erectile dysfunction.

Potency depends upon the **autonomic nervous system** to function appropriately in directing the blood to different parts of the body. Internal sensors regulate most of our body systems to keep conditions optimal for the body's preservation.

The body at rest from labor and defence employs the **parasympathetic system** to keep arterial blood in the central parts of the body, thereby supporting healthy nourishment. Digestion is activated to extract and supply the body cells with nutrients. The heart, trunk, and lungs are assured the flow of blood with nutrients to build up reserves of strength. That way, the storehouse will be ready to deliver spare resources to the peripheral parts of the body when needed.

. The **sympathetic system** is the agent that defends the total body. It prepares the body to meet threats. In an emergency or threat from the environment, the sympathetic system triggers the alarm. It acts antagonistically with the parasympathetic and shuts down non-essential body functions.

The sympathetic system increases the flow of blood to the peripheral parts of the body, to the long muscles that will do the fighting. The arms are readied for fighting and the legs for running. Potency is not required in battle so reproductive functions are shut down. The reduced blood flow to the peripheral arterioles of the penis will help reduce the loss of blood in case of a wound or other injury, but this causes temporary impotence. If you are in a fighting situation there is no problem. If you are mounting a sweetheart, impotence can be a big problem!

* * * * *

The key to understanding deviant behavior lies in searching out what threatens a person and how he defends himself against it. Defences focus on removing or disguising the corporeal nature of if fear or guilt is associated with them. The operating principle is that safety can only be obtained by distancing one's self from the threat.

Raw, crude sex is seldom the objective for us weirdos. We live in a world of obscurity-- veiled dreams and infantile needs. We voyeurs are seldom out for a quick biological connection; we may be even frightened by a successful one.

We are intimidated when a target turns on us and invites us to enter the front door like a man-- that's entirely outside the game plan. Despite our aggressive forays in our imaginations, we are reluctant, reticent, and shy. Voyeurs are hardly the kind of sex-crazed beast imagined for the public. Assaulters and rapists are never accepted in our club. We are sexual deviants but not monsters.

When a person's body is prepared for "fight or flight", it is not ready to "feed or fornicate." The key to understanding impotence lies in the childhood experiences of sinning.

All of us start life .enjoying life's pleasures. We depend upon our parents to limit wisely those sources of pleasure-- they teach us what is forbidden. Few dour priests waste their time teaching us what is pleasing. We soon learn the constraints glorified by the Bible so that we can please our parents-- we become good Catholics.

Mounting any woman requires self-assurance, whether she is a romantic heroine or a common street whore. Some men engage only with prostitutes because they are less threatening. Pleasing a partner takes guts, and skills for interacting with others-- some men never become experienced in those arts.

You may have a record of good experiences in mounting your partners or you may have failed. If you did fail, your masculinity is brought into question.

One explanation for failing with women is that their bodies are unappealing. But that would suggest a preference for males, and that implies homosexuality. If no manipulations can restore potency then the trouble will have been amplified.

A slap on the cheek of the nursing infant is a good deterrent if he bites the nipple. However, he will associate the disapproval with the feeling of his head pressed against a breast. If that occurs daily then it can affect him for the remainder of his life so that he is wary of close cuddling.

Parents hold to the convenient fiction that whatever an adult has forgotten about his childhood couldn't have been important. Put simply. "It was a long time ago and well forgotten." Nothing could be further from the truth. Ignoring the cumulative effect of daily learning produces seriously maladaptive personalities.

The earlier the experiences, the more potent they are, because the child's world is so small, and he is so vulnerable. Picture the 6-year-old boy standing before his father, who is always passing judgements. Father questions the boy in harsh tones and the little boy quivers. He has never learned to stand up to authority; in fact, he has been taught to be submissive. Under those conditions, he learns to withdraw and to conceal his secret self.

His reaction would be the same even were the scene transferred to being confronted by his mother. He would lie, apologize and back down. These same parents will want him to be self-confident and assertive when he starts dating young ladies. Later, they will wonder why he is not the CEO of the company he works for as a stock clerk. They don't want a wimp for a son, but they may have created one.

Sonny knows full-well that his father is an aggressive male and that he could never dare compete with him. Should competition with another mate over a girlfriend arise, he will slouch off.

A chance to score with a girl will be threatening because it places him in a situation where he may fail.

Lacking a girlfriend and a normal outlet for sex, he may turn to his less threatening male buddies. Rewards from interacting with guys are fewer but so are the threats.

He may manage to establish a trial sexual relationship with a girl but he is likely to spoil it by reacting defensively. He feels threatened by intimate contacts so he avoids them. He feels that he is being naughty and he tries to limit his pleasure so he needn't feel so guilty. He will be unable to obtain the real joy that he should be able to experience. The closer a relationship becomes, the more he struggles to be free of it.

The copulating male has to overcome two points of vulnerability. When he climbs up on top, he is conspicuously sinning, even more so than during foreplay. His unconscious is telling him, "Now you're being really bad and you should be punished." He is expected to behave like a man but he doesn't feel like one. There is plenty of time for regrets to set in before he reaches orgasm, so he may discontinue and blame his partner for it.

His focus will shift from enticing his partner to his own self-conscious performance:

"Is it getting soft? Maybe we shouldn't be doing this. What if I can't come? What if she tells her friends that I'm not a man? Maybe I'm too small. What if somebody sees us? Maybe I shouldn't have done myself yesterday-- I may not have any more juices left."

On a deeper level of consciousness, he is confusing his partner's sexuality with his mother's:

"Does Mother really do this with Father? Surly they don't do it often, because it's such a bad thing to do. I wonder if it feels good for Father. I wonder if sons and mothers ever do it together (God forgive me for my evil thoughts!)"

It's a wonder that any men are able to complete the coital act with a loved one. Many have to use a debased partner so that the comparison with the pure mother is repressed further. This pushing away the love object explains a lot of instances of wife abuse.

Physical and verbal assault may be necessary to diminish the female partner so that she no longer resembles Mother. He may introduce suffering to pay in advance for his pleasure-- which makes him a sadist or a masochist.

Others can complete the game only by engaging in "perverted actions." Some will get through a degrading session with the mate dressing as a nurse or schoolteacher to take the responsibility for the conjugation. Submission is necessary and may reach the point where ejaculation can be reached only after he is whipped. If he pays the price of his sin in advance, he can have a free ride. Handcuffs can help an impotent man avoid the blame for an encounter by making him the helpless victim.

You probably see where this discourse is headed. The voyeur usually suffers from at least partial impotence during his active lifetime. He starts life trying to juggle the basic joy of sexual gratification with the ever-increasing neurotic guilt and anxiety of trying to establish adult sexual relations.

Sexual action requires activation of the male's parasympathetic system. Introducing any threat or danger provokes the sympathetic system into action and suppresses the parasympathetic.

The voyeur is, "Up the creek without a paddle." He will avoid the whole scene of missionary sex in the future. He will seek outlets like viewing Playboy and pornography because they are less threatening. The voyeur's activates take on a sneaky character:

In a typical case, a voyeur will fall in step behind some young chick walking along the sidewalk. He will feel the throbbing under his coat. He will reach down with the wish that he could relieve himself, but the best he can do is to keep on following her and enjoy the excitement that the situation brings. She completes her journey as she reaches her apartment or car. He won't finish until he is inside his own lodging. A blast of uninhibited release confirms his successful application of the virtues of voyeurism.

The voyeur usually keeps the target at a distance, thus minimizing the threats to him. He deliberately choses inanimate targets or ones far enough away to be non-threatening. Indeed, if a woman target catches him in the act, he probably will run away in fright, especially if she looks like she wants to join in the game.

Impotence is not a hopeless problem for the voyeur unless he displays his body to a lady friend and she shows disgust. Such an experience would be disheartening. If the feelings leading to impotence continue to exist, he may have to look for other types of targets to increase the sexual attraction or diminish the threat. The voyeur is an experimenter not a quitter. By trying to reduce the threat from adult sexuality, he may be tempted into the paedophile minefield of using children.

Deep hostility toward women can be dangerous when mixed with impotence. Violence may have to become part of the scene for him to be able to get it off. Rapists and serial killers usually have some aggressive voyeurism in their make-up.

Their means of gratification can become so extreme that the public thinks that these monsters are "crazy." They are not-- they are only irresponsible members of society, who should be incarcerated or executed. They are individuals, who have never learned society's limits, and they must be prevented from committing their crimes.

IMMOKOLEE PERIOD

Narrated by Abraham Murray

IMMOKOLEE TECH

I spent my first five years establishing myself in the Miami Beach community. I never enjoyed life more than when I was one of the really cool guys on the scene. It was during that period that I developed my skills as a five-star voyeur.

Although I spent my fun weekends in Miami Beach, I was glad to have another foothold in Immokalee. It was a couple of months before a Latina fieldworker named Selena put her hooks into me. I had never before known the endlessness of sex with a Caribbean Latina. She moved in to live with me and we had sex day and night.

Selena smothered me. I realized that this absurd emphasis on intercourse was routed in her insecurity. Later, an experienced colleague explained to me that the Latin girls try to keep their lovers drained so that they won't drift away from home. While Selena was fucking me in Immokalee, I still had to play house with Bunny in Miami Beach on weekends.

That was a bit of a strain for me, and I had this problem with Selena. She was too focussed on copulation-- a worthy goal for a woman looking to establish a home and have babies. Unfortunately, her interests differed from my own. I was irrevocably dedicated to foreplay and devious gratifications. Selena had the rigid Catholic view that all fun should be devoted to coital action that could bring forth children for the glory of the Church.

The parties in Immokalee were drunken Latino orgies. There was lots of kissing and hugging-- good family love with an occasional "feel." We used to attend parties in Immokalee that spilled over into my Miami Beach condo. I preferred to keep my two playgrounds separate but it wasn't always possible.

By the time the party was transported to my Miami residence everybody either had passed out or had moved closer to my ideas of fun. Clothing was optional, but sort of frowned upon. You could just sit around nude or you could make a pretence of wearing a swimming suit that soon became too tight to tolerate.

I did a careful inspection of each body that entered my domain. It didn't matter much if I saw girls through a peek hole or openly. Anyhow, if they pissed in my main bathroom, then I knew about all their assets. Others stripped to make my assessment both easy and fun. I had an occasional orgasm but the real kick came out of driving my herd along the glory path. I love to see others having fun.

Of course Bunny and Selena never did get along-- I knew I couldn't hang on to both of them. After a few months the three of us were tired of the hassle and Bunny sent Selena packing to stay back in Immokalee. Selena used to pester me to hook up with her again, but I refused to succumb to her overtures. Eventually she took up with a Cuban farm worker. The last I heard they were working along the Arizona-Mexico border.

I created a positive, bachelor-type image on the Beach. Minor troubles with the law were mollified by my friends-- the influential guys. These guys had been guests at my parties and I had fixed them up with my surplus lady friends. Five glorious years passed quickly and pleasantly, but I had neglected to develop my academic standing.

During my five years in Immokalee I saw many progressive changes. Glass and steel structures replaced the old barn-like classroom buildings. New concrete roads and bridges replaced the crumbling, rock-compacted causeways that used to run through the surrounding swampland.

The locals shared their pride in building a progressive institution. The Board of Governors no longer was a laughing stock; they had earned the respect of the academic community. I was proud to be a member of the faculty.

My extended sun-and-fun holiday was coming to an end. It was time to shift my priorities to getting tenure at the College. I always had intended to have a foot in both communities-- it was safer that way. If I fouled up in one place I could escape to the other.

I maintained a working relation with the Church by going to holiday masses in both of my two parishes. I contributed annually to each parish and the priests knew me as a respectable Catholic. If I were disgraced in one parish, I might still be able to get character references from the other.

I had strong supporters in Miami but I was being evaluated in Immokalee, and I was worried. I didn't want a shift to academic matters to limit my freewheeling style of operating in Miami Beach.

The Chairman of our Board of Governors of Immokalee Tech was very conservative, so of course, we didn't see eye-to-eye on anything. He never did like me. He was jealous of my youth and I was not submissive to his authority, either as Board Chairman or as church leader. However, he was a businessman, a plantation owner, and so he had a keen, practical orientation.

He spent his whole life bargaining so he didn't know any subtle ways of operating. He told me that he would see that I got tenure if I brought in a grant of $200,000. If it reached half a million, he would see that I was appointed Chairman of a new Latin American Studies Center.

It so happened that at that time I was friendly with a family of Venezuelan farm workers. When I was visiting with them one night, I brought up my problem of needing to obtain a grant in order to assure my continued appointment.

An older member of the family said, "My uncle is the Assistant Secretary of Cultural Affairs in

Washington." I told myself, "One should not despise good fortune when it comes or else the next time good luck just may pass you by." A phone call to the Secretary of State's cultural affairs office evoked an unexpectedly positive response. The Department had an open budget item for a study of Venezuelan indigenous languages that would expire within a year.

With a lot of fast stepping, I persuaded the Department of Cultural Affairs to consider a proposal that I was drafting for just such a project. I immediately mobilized my forces and focussed my efforts on producing a grant proposal of major importance.

Four weeks later I submitted an application for, "A study of the language of the Waranii tribes of Lower Venezuela." Chief Investigator: Abraham Murray, PhD.

Shit! What did I get myself into? I would have to hide my ignorance and provide convincing cover for the grant. I had always been living on the edge, fending off the civil authorities. Now I found myself up against all the suspicious bookkeepers in Washington, and there are a hell of a lot of them.

It was a repetition of my old masturbatory fears. They would know about me just by looking in my eyes. Even if the reviews went well, all my current fun on the tropical beach would be displaced by boring documents, and meetings with stupid committees. Shit! What had I gotten myself into?

It took a couple of weeks but then I started seeing the positive side of switching my attention over to the grant. The budget would make it possible for me to go to exciting South America. I was getting satiated with my Miami Beach life, anyhow. Life was too good; I no longer appreciated it, so the change would do me good.

* * * * *

Florida Senator Charlie Johnson's office in Tallahassee phoned me to arrange an appointment with him. He seated me in a plush chair and offered me a big old cigar. He kept on addressing me as "Son" in his syrupy Southern drawl. I'd rather be the son of the Devil than be a distant relative of his!

He saved the good things for himself, like the shrewd politician he was. He gladly took the credit for making the grant available to me. I hid my annoyance and thanked him. I was glad to have the grant approved but I resented having to receive the award at the Senator's hands. His contribution involved sitting in a couple of committee meetings and shaking hands with the real sources of funding.

It would be a year later that I found out what the real sources of funding were. They obscured their identity by getting the State Department to administer the project. They wanted to hide their real motives.

It turned out that the whole project was disguised as part of the Agency for International Development program (AID). The little scab that I was scratching had pseudopodia reaching out in many directions, that the public didn't need to know about. It turned out that my grant was just a small part of a 20-year-long program that was hatched up by the State Department and the CIA to penetrate deeply into the Venezuelan interior.

The Florida Institute of Summer Languages (FISL) often cooperated with the State Department. The FISL provided cover for American spies, gathering field intelligence, and was the vehicle for religious proselytizing.

FISI's sources of funding remained obscure but the State Department got together a hundred million dollars to make the long-term program a success. The secret sources were the CIA, the military, and the oil conglomerates. Even corporations that had contracts with our government to supply mercenaries, added to the fund.

Why were all these agencies suddenly interested in Venezuela? Well, it wasn't much of a surprise. The Bible thumpers had been going there and elsewhere for decades. They were preparing to play a major role when the Day of Glory arrived. They wanted to be the center of influence. The government took advantage of everyone who traveled from the States to Venezuela on State Department business. Each had to smuggle in 50 copies of the Bible translated into Yanomami, a native language.

The CIA was always on the lookout for places to stash spies and develop local informants. They needed citizens like us to pay their informers and to recruit local agents to promote political dissent. The federal government always needed help in running the world-- diplomats and bookkeepers couldn't manage it alone.

Isolated places like Venezuela were growing increasingly important to the industrialized world. Venezuela had huge petroleum reserves hidden in the jungle. We wanted to be the principal extractors of all their mineral wealth. At the very least, we wanted to make sure that our enemies didn't control the country's natural resources.

My academic future was assured, even advanced by the grant. Now all I had to do was convince everybody that I was an expert on the ways of the Waranii people. Even getting to meet one of them would be a progressive step.

CARACAS, VENEZUELA

I sat quietly in my tourist class seat and forked over my hard-earned American dollars for some rum cokes. When federal inspectors audit grants they can't examine every detail. Knowing that, I avoided setting off warning lights of extravagance in the hope that I would be trusted when I spent more freely in future matters.

I hoped that I would disarm the auditors by not going first class, I would store up good will and put them off my trail. There would be plenty of opportunities to charge the grant for first-class hotels and restaurants. I even should be able to use grant money to pay for the companionship of some temporary help.

I arrived in Caracas with a small suitcase and a copy of the grant agreement. The 50 bibles were shipped as cargo, so I had to make sure that they were delivered to the embassy by courier.

The grant period was to expire soon so there had been no time to secure American personnel. However, I always look after my friends. I persuaded my old major professor and friend, Dr. Milo to go to Venezuela with me. His competence and standing in the field of social sciences justified hiring him to consult on the grant project. He managed to secure a substitute to teach his Immokalee summer-term classes, and I   was able to cover his expenses. I paid his summer salary from the grant. Milo was to arrive a few days after me to begin his consultation service.

The emissary from the American Embassy was there to meet me on arrival at Caracas. He took me to a hotel in the capitol city. The courier from the embassy arranged in advance for a guide named Juan to meet us there to see to our further needs. We were welcomed warmly at the hotel, partly because it was owned by Juan's brother.

We went to the bar to celebrate my safe arrival. I found myself surrounded by people. I couldn't establish whether they were Juan's relatives or were staff that we hired to meet my needs. I was lost, a babe in the woods. I knew it and I didn't care-- I had Juan to look after me.

I tossed back another shot of Cacique brand aged rum and I smiled at the partiers. I was not a total boor-- I shook hands or nodded to each one of them, successively. At the time I didn't realize how completely different my life would have to be in my new situation. I didn't appreciate fully how lucky I was to encounter subordinates who would be so helpful with my endeavors in a strange world.

I had adapted to the Caribbean life-style from living in the Miami area for five years, but I had never been immersed so completely. There had been nights of Matacumbe JuJu on the beach but even then, the next morning we returned to our own sane, daytime lives. I hadn't seen anything yet!

I rested up all the next day. The second night I got to meet my Caracas driver, Ramon. He came to the hotel to take me out to familiarize me with the neighborhood bars. He knew what things interested the Gringo visitors.

We walked a couple of blocks over to the Street of Prostitutes, and ordered rum cokes. I didn't know it at the time but the owner was his cousin. What the hell, everybody down here is somebody's cousin!

That was when I first met Eva. She was the tall languid form that emerged from the crowd on the sidewalk to capture my attention. Juan called her over to join us. She was his cousin, too. With one more rum coke, I began to feel like somebody's cousin, also. Her smile was so enchanting I couldn't take my eyes off her. To be honest, most of the time my eyes were on her boobs more than on than her smile.

From the corner of my eye, I noticed a vague human form slip up to our table and pick up my glass. I heard the greeting, *Salud*, and it only took a second for him to replace the empty glass on my table. He smiled as I turned to look at him and he wished me a good evening.

I was incensed at his audacity, but then the magic of the venue started to penetrate my thick skull. I could act like an outraged *patron* or I could enter into the spirit of life as it really is down here. This stranger had shared my drink and welcomed me to Caracas. Perhaps he was one of my cousins, too!

I had salary line-items in the grant that needed to be used. I eagerly hired Eva, once I established that she had completed her secondary school studies. She became my Urban Coordinator right then and there. We had another round to celebrate her appointment. By then I was in an expansive mood so I hired Cousin Juan as Supervising Technical Coordinator.

I had no illusion that I had bought these people outright, nor did I desire to. I was determined to maintain as reasonable a distance between employer and employee as possible in that setting. I always try to follow the old maxim, "Don't shit where you eat!" I would try to refrain from physical contact with them, but that didn't mean that I couldn't enjoy their company.

My mentor, Milo came to Caracas three days after my own arrival. I was waiting for him so that we could penetrate the interior together. I scheduled our flight to the jungle so Milo would get two good nights of sleep in Caracas and still have time to orient himself to the city. That also gave him time to become familiar with our grant assistants.

This first trip to the interior was for familiarization rather than for gathering data, so I brought all my main team members. We picked up a translator, who was able to accompany us. We were looking for a Waranii, who spoke Spanish or English fluently. Finding a good one would have made our job too easy, but it was not to be.

Wazu was one of a rare breed. He was a Waranii, who spoke the Yanomami language. He had been living in Caracas for a year, so he knew a few words of Spanish, and even some English. Of course we couldn't help joking among ourselves about his name- "Up the wazoo!" (I know-- you're thinking I'm not a nice person).

Milo and I, along with my four employees, went to the airport to catch a local flight. It was scheduled to depart at noon for the jungle city of Puerto Ayacucho, Venezuela. We planned to make this city our base of operations in the wilderness.

Puerto Ayacucho is an old outpost trading-center on the mighty Orinoco River. The river is one of the largest tributaries from the Amazon Basin. It drains the large expanse of wet tropical lands of the interior of Venezuela, Columbia, and the Guianas. Many different tribes live along this long, meandering river, but we were interested only in the Waranii. Unlike their Yanomami neighbors, they gathered in small clusters of huts rather than in the form of a real tribal village. They made scattered camps along the river.

* * * * *

Everything went smoothly until we reached the boarding gate. We had our equipment and luggage on board and we looked forward to sitting back in our seats and resting up for the hassle that would accompany deplaning. We couldn't be that lucky!

An officious guard blocked my entrance to the boarding gate. He looked me up and down arrogantly. He asked for our passports and then went into the act that he so loved to play. "Where is your permit from our Minister to visit the interior? I pretended not to speak Spanish so he pushed us into an inspection room to wait.

Eventually a suit from the Minister of the Interior arrived. He introduced himself as an assistant to the Minister. He looked over our papers and clucked his tongue, "When will you Americans learn to follow protocol in our country?" I feigned innocence but got the point that his visit had to do with our lack of a permit to visit the interior.

Briefings back in the States prepared me for situations just like this. I knew that you don't mess with the Department of the Interior. They control the natural resources of the country. *El Presidente* rules by the consent of the Minister of the Interior, who holds office under the patronage of the Gringos.

The aide didn't beat around the bush any further. He declared that he could issue us a permit, but that it would cost twice as much because of the inconvenience of our having failed to obtain one in advance. The upfront price was $100.00 USD, so either we would come up with double or we would be denied boarding. I asked him if there would still be time to catch our flight if we had to wait for a permit.

He smiled grimly and professed that he would like to be of service. "I am sorry. I realize how inconvenient it would be to miss this flight. The flights to Puerto Ayacucho only depart three times a week, so you would be delayed two days at least. If you would like to donate another $200.00 to our Indian Charities, then the rules might be bent, not broken." After I paid him $400.00, everybody was most courteous and we boarded and were on our way.

After flying over God's verdant jungle for two hours, we arrived in the middle of the afternoon when every sensible person still was napping or just waking up. We were received with minimal ceremony.

I had spent a few nights in Miami brushing up on my Spanish, but. I could have saved myself the trouble. Even our guides had to communicate with most of the locals through grunts and gestures.

What I learned on my visit to the Waranii villages certainly was not worth the taxpayers' dollars. Half an hour's reading of the pertinent material in Wikipedia would provide all the information we could get from those difficult people.

I did learn something quite incidentally. The almost total nudity in the village convinced me that one must maintain obscurity and mystery about sex if you desire full enjoyment. Nothing diminishes sexual pleasure more than satiation.

The assortment of exciting boobs surrounding me soon converted into smelly, sweaty bodies in need of a good dunking in the river. After seeing boobs everywhere, I no longer looked, peeked, or even cared about them. I wanted to be free from them, forever. I couldn't believe that I used to be aroused by boobs waving in my face. It was like giving a kid all the ice cream he can eat until he vomits-- it cures him of the craving.

I no longer could identify residuals of voyeuristic impulses in me. I didn't want to sneak around huts or stalk young ladies. I thought to myself, "Is this what it's like to be dead, to care about nothing?"

* * * * *

The local Waranii chief welcomed us the day after we arrived. The meeting began with a vigorous shaking of hands (actually, it was a grasping of forearms) which continued with lots of grunts and smiles. Words in Waranii and occasional Spanish could be heard, but they were superfluous and rather useless for communicating.

We had anticipated the awkward gaps in communication, the long silences that were inevitable. Juan unpacked a liter of rum to lubricate the tongues. After finishing a second bottle, we had to excuse ourselves so we could take naps. Everybody in the jungle took a siesta. Even the sounds of the wilderness were muted.

The locals accompanied us to the larger common building where we would be staying. It was constructed completely with materials from the jungle. The floor was elevated from the ground on stilts to keep out the snakes. Parts of the floor were covered over with bamboo with scattered reed mats spread on top.

Sleep didn't come easily, tired as we were. Everything was so different and came at us so fast that we didn't have time to process it. I never slept in a hammock before, and believe me, it was a challenge.

My assistants arranged to put together a meal of sorts. It consisted of fish over some ground vegetable mush. All the unspent grant money couldn't buy a meal in this isolated green dessert that would be fit a Gringo. I got used to sleeping in a hammock but I never could stomach the food. I lost 10 pounds during my first weeklong visit to the wilderness.

The next day the noises of the jungle woke us up. We had nothing scheduled, so we took some coffee and ate some more of the vegetable mush. It turned out to be from the cassava plant, the starchy root that was a staple in the local diet. It soon found favor with those of us, who didn't want to starve. We even learned to swallow a cassava beer, called *chicha*.

After breakfast we wandered around. A local with a blowpipe beckoned us to follow him into the jungle.. He entered a path with us in tow. We heard the monkeys chattering away in the trees while they enjoyed their all-day breakfast.

We didn't realize why our guide was taking us deeper into the jungle, until he slowly raised his 10-foot-long blowpipe to his lips. There was a popping noise followed by a shriek in the canopy of trees, and then came the thud of a howler monkey hitting the ground.

Our local hunting guide tied the two arms of the monkey together around his neck to carry him back to the camp. The monkey was so hideous in his death rictus, that I knew my evening meal would be vegetarian. Nevertheless, we were greeted with accolades upon returning with the day's animal protein that would be shared by the tribe.

It was playtime when we returned to camp, so our hosts gave each of us a blowgun and darts. They staked out a target of grasses and fibers tied together to form a bundle. We huffed and puffed, and entertained the locals with our ineptitude. We tired of being losers so we looked around for something else to occupy us.

Eva picked up a penis guard laying in the corner of our hut, and dared me to don it. These penis guards are like a man's jockstrap and serve a similar purpose. The shields are made of a mixture of rough vines and softer fibers of straw. They cover the penis and a vine secures it around the waist. They come to a point at the end and extend upward, to rest against the abdomen. They look sort of like a straw penis with an erection.

I had been too good for too long and was just waiting for a chance to be naughty. I took Eva up on her dare. I stripped nude and then wrapped the penis guard around my waist. I walked around proudly with a projection in front that was twice its usual size.

Eva came over to me coyly and slid her hand up and under the guard. She asked me, "Is it comfortable?" She really didn't want an answer. She reached around my back and untied the vine. Then we had sex just as the natives do, right there before God and a few other spectators. The prohibition of sexual relations with employees is nothing more than a rule, and rules are to be broken.

After we returned to Caracas I was able to consult with a professor from the university. He explained the reasons behind covering the penis:

> Keep others from envying the man's vigor and size, thus invoking impotence.

> Protect the member from falling debris or from vines catching on it and tearing it off.

> Retaining the spirits in the sack so that they won't spill out.

It was on the first trip that I had the chance to learn about the hallucinogenic, psychedelic plant, named *ayahwhasca*. Generally, only the shaman (witch doctor) drinks the ayahwhasca infusion.

Taking this drug is a very serious matter because it is very strong and the physical effects can last for more than a day. The experiences of locals with the drug have a very strong influence on their lives.

The locals believe that the visions seen during its use are reflections of the true world, not the everyday illusionary ones. They conduct their lives based upon what is revealed in the trance.

Outsiders, who have experienced the effects, warn others not to attempt ingesting it because it is too potent. It is better to stick to LSD and the peyote mushroom for milder psychedelic experiences.

Secrets of the world are revealed by the drug and hidden enemies are disclosed. Some Amazonian tribes make preemptive raids on their neighbors when they learn from a trance that the neighbors really are enemies. After raiding their village, they sever the heads and shrink them. Then they tie the neck tissue together to keep the spirits from escaping. As far as I knew there were no headhunters in the Venezuelan jungle, at least I hoped not.

The chief told us that the shaman was going to go on a psychedelic trip that afternoon and we were invited to witness the ceremony. We went to the shaman's tent and sat opposite him in a semicircle. He smoked rolled-up tobacco leaves that were too rough and loosely packed to be called cigars.

He blew smoke to the four cardinal points and he blew it in our faces, and even across our bodies. It was his way of controlling the spirits to make them go where he wished, and to stay out of our bodies. He continued to chant and blow smoke even when he was too intoxicated to stand up,

After he vomited a couple of times, he just sat there with a stupid grin on his face. For several hours he was unaware of our presence. We were bored to death, and left him to his visions when he rolled over on his side with his eyes staring,.

As with other psychedelic drugs, it's what is going on inside the subject that matters, not the exterior world. Rich as that inner experience is, it is hard to share with another. That's why I have included an admirable effort of a Western user to describe the inner events.

According to him,

> "It will make you cry, vomit, and make you feel amazing... It was as if the universe were wrapping me in giant mutating arms and filling me full of love. I saw God, and I was God, and everything was God.

> For most of this part, the good part, I just lay on my back with my eyes closed in a little euphoric bubble. And if only that could have lasted, because pretty soon, the bad part kicked in.

> In one incident after the next, I revisited traumatic chapters of my childhood. It played out like some celebrity retrospective-- only instead of showing the best clips from my long career, I was forced to witness the moments that had bruised me most. I was in the womb feeling my family's stress, in school running from bullies, and in my teenage bedroom listening to

Smashing Pumpkins while writing poetry with rhymes like "blunt knives" and "short lives."

In the middle of this trip down misery lane, I broke out in feverish sweat and felt the need to puke. But like I said, I was worried my container wouldn't handle my load, so I got up and wobbled to the bathroom. My stomach was a mess, but I couldn't puke, so I tried to shit."

Conor Creighton, 2014

The day before our return to Puerto Ayacucho, we had the opportunity to join a local celebration. Even to this day, I don't know what we were celebrating. Perhaps the Waranii were happy at getting rid of us stupid Gringos.

I had heard of the Indian beverage made of manioc root (cassava) but never tasted it before. This native equivalent of Western beer is called *chicha* and has similar, mild intoxicating qualities:

The women of the tribe dig up the root and then boil it all day long to get rid of its poison. It softens in the process. It is further pulverized by the women, who, in chewing it, add enzymes from their saliva. Finally, the women spit it into a vessel where it will ferment. That completes the process of breaking the mash down into a milky white liquid.

The Waranii follow their own social customs. The serving of chicha to a guest involves a ritual of hospitality, the opposite of that in the civilized world.

The wife takes the first generous swallow herself, before handing the bowl to her husband. He in turn takes a large portion before offering it to guests.

This is more than a custom-- it is a survival tactic. The rate of women murdering their husbands is very high in the jungle. Visitors are at risk because there is no virtue in protecting an enemy, who is inflicting mortal curses on you. The protective bond of "Breaking bread together" counts for little when dealing with an enemy.

* * * * *

We left with a bigger Waranii vocabulary than when we arrived. We knew Hello, Good-Bye, and Thank You. The next trip would be for gathering vocabulary data, but we could wait until then to lengthen our list. Now all we needed to know was "Good-Bye." We headed up river to Puerto Ayacucho and semi-civilization.

We arrived late afternoon and checked in. I asked my crew what they wanted to do first, sleep, drink, or eat. They all opted for a table of edible food that didn't stare back at you.

Some days later we boarded the plane for Caracas and sighed with relief. Our first trip into the jungle had gone without incident and that made me overconfident. Nothing abroad is as easy as you expect it to be. There must be some kind of law operating: "When things are going too well, then somebody has to fuck things up to restore the natural imbalance."

We were back in Caracas for several weeks with nothing to do but drink or get into trouble. Milo was good at both and had the time to indulge himself.

I was glad I was able to bring Milo to Venezuela. He was not only good company-- he was fun to watch. It had been thirty years since he left Bulgaria to take up residency in the USA. During those thirty years he never left the "Land of Plenty." He thought he had seen the last of poverty and misery.

The poor city districts and the jungle camps of the Indians reminded him of his own days of impoverishment. That aspect of the trip was a downer for both of us. He drank too much rum and felt much too sorry for himself.

When he drank, his tongue loosened, and from his mouth came the curses that he had been storing up all his life. He complained---

The Orthodox Greeks had never been suitable masters since the days of glorious Macedonian supremacy. The Greeks no longer brought peace and order to their occupied lands. Those who invaded Bulgaria were like the goats from the mountains in which they originated. They were gruff and wild. They had grown to resemble the members of their herds more than they did citizens of the renowned city-states from two millennia ago.

Milo cursed the victorious Turks for taking over his village and making them strangers in their own birthplace. The Turks cursed the Bulgarians and labelled them infidels. The Turks treated the local people with contempt. They belittled them and tried to make them feel guilty because they were not born to Muslim parents. Milo's people were liberated from the cruel life of being serfs in the lord's feudal estates only to become miserable peasants in the glorious Turkish Empire.

The disruptions in Milo's life made him bitter. He was a geographically displaced person, who was marginalized further by a heterosexual society. The injuries to his soul could never be cured by the comfortable life in America, or by shouting his furious protests against world injustices.

It turned out that I unwittingly completed the destruction of Milo when I brought him to Venezuela. "No good deed goes unpunished."

At least we had a final month together before the tragedy.. Or was it a tragedy? Maybe it was just Milo's destiny to bleed to death in a Caracas alley. That tragedy, like so many others, could be traced back to its beginning-- love.

Milo fell in love with a Caracas boy that he found wandering the streets. They satisfied their lusts for several weeks but then they were exposed. The boy's uncle was irate. He demanded satisfaction from the Gringo.

The uncle's friends urged caution. Killing a Gringo was very bad for tourism and that would bring down the wrath of the police and the American Embassy.

The uncle backed off a bit and said that he would consider a monetary settlement. Milo learned that the uncle waned $1,000 to compensate for the loss of the family honor and Milo was incensed for the boy's sake. He turned righteous and wanted to meet the uncle in person so he could beat the shit out of him.

They did meet in a dark Caracas alley but Milo didn't get a chance to beat the shit out of anybody, ever again. The flash of the machete blade unburdened Milo's soul and he died quietly and peacefully. The American Embassy was notified and asked what should be done with the body.

Nobody wanted the disruption brought on by a dead American; it would be an embarrassment. The police were advised unofficially that the Americans wanted to avoid a diplomatic hassle. The Embassy didn't want a fuss made about the killing of an American because that would enrage the American newspaper readers, who would demand justice. Nor did they want the embarrassment that would accompany the disclosure of a homosexual lover's quarrel involving an American.

The sanitizing experts in the national police took over. They were well experienced in making people disappear. Mangrove swamps were available there, just like they were back home in south Florida. The Embassy issued a formal explanation of the tragedy:

"Professor Milo Yankowitz, who was an avid fisherman, was believed to have fallen overboard while fishing offshore for dolphin. Funeral services were held in absentia at the Embassy so that his friends could pay their last respects.

The whole affair shook me up. I was alarmed that losing a dear friend was treated so casually by our representatives abroad. Death and murder were hitting too close to home. I wasn't sure whether I could stick with this game, and not bolt for the relative safety of Florida.

The rest of us didn't have much to do but sit around. Juan and Eva seemed to hang out together. I never could figure out the relationship between them. It would be useless to ask them because they would lie. At first I thought that Juan was Eva's pimp, but later he called her cousin and treated her with respect. Maybe he was both-- a businessman employing his cousin as a worker in the Street of Prostitutes.

Ramon was available on call, but he spent his days playing dominoes and drinking coffee where other locals congregated. I decided to put Wazu to work after a week of sitting around. I had to show some tangible progress with the grant. All of us assembled at my hotel.

No vocabulary chart of the Waranii spoken language was available so we set about making one. That took only one day because we were able to copy on paper the sounds produced by Wazu. He made the successive sounds and then we wrote them down in the appropriate phonetic characters.

That was the only tangible result of our first foray into the jungle, but it was something to impress my sponsors with. We no longer needed to expend energy on serious matters, so we rested up for another week. That gave me time to think about what to do next.

The sponsors expected us to return to the Waranii camp so we could produce a dictionary of 100 important words from their language. I was the Chief Investigator for the project, so it was my responsibility to determine which words in Waranii merited inclusion in our collection. Before I left Florida I was given a list of words considered important by my sponsor. I was encouraged to include as many of them as possible in my dictionary.

The sponsor's list "got lost" on the way to the Miami airport. I remember a few of the atrocious suggestions: Savior, Redeemer, Resurrection. That's all I can remember offhand; I'm doing well to recall that many.

* * * * *

Everything was prepared and made ready for our second visit to the Waranii. We managed to assemble our field gear and board the flight to Puerto Ayacucho.

After arriving in Ayacucho, we stayed in a hotel the first night and then took the river trip down to the small settlement we visited earlier.

We were met at the landing bank of the encampment by all the males of the tribe. They stood there in a hostile stance with their spears at ready. Even the little boys had adopted scowls that warned us not to land. Wazu was one of their own, so they allowed him to disembark to talk with them.

They visited together for half an hour or so before Wazu returned. Since Wazu spoke very bad English and Spanish, so we couldn't be sure about what he was telling us. It seemed like the Waranii were saying that we brought evil spirits into their camp.

As near as we could tell, one of their maidens became very ill after our previous visit. She was healthy before we came so it was logical that somebody in our party must have put a curse on her. Besides, three pigs died without reason and this confirmed that we had brought evil spirits to their camp.

There is no sense in trying to argue with people, who have made up their minds. We never left the boat; we just headed back up-river to Puerto Ayacucho. We weren't out to win any battles.

We anticipated a joyous reception by the Puerto Ayacucho hotel staff because Uncle Sam was footing the bill. Sadly, it didn't work out that way. We were greeted with the thrusts of rifles as we clamored out up on the landing dock at Puerto Ayacucho. We never reached the town; we were hustled off to a military camp and each of us was shoved into separate interrogation rooms.

There was no Hilton on the military base and if there were, the comfortable suites wouldn't be wasted on deceitful Gringos like us. They knew enough to keep us Gringo spies separated. They didn't want us to develop a cover story to explain why we were on Venezuelan soil "advancing the enemy's interests."

It may be possible to prove a person is guilty of being a spy but to prove the reverse is impossible. The pleasant holiday that we anticipated turned into a nightmare. We had to share a large cell with a bunch of other inmates, who were sick, discouraged, and disgusting.

I kept my head and recalled what I had learned from TV dramas. We were hostages so the captors must have wanted something from us. We had to find out what they wanted and exchange it for our freedom.

It turned out that the squadron stationed in Puerto Ayacucho felt ignored and neglected by their superiors in Caracas. The Caracas leaders suspected that the ever-present insurgents had offered some of the Puerto Ayacucho field officers better postings in a new revolutionary government. The officers in the outpost had to use our capture to prove their loyalty to the government, so that they would get more pledges of support.

Everybody wanted to work out a package that would get Caracas' approval, if not their blessing. At times like this, everybody looks for enemies to blame-- the CIA, DEA, and AID agencies. America had too many covert operations to hide.

Only the previous month, the Americans sent in a squadron of black operators. They tried to kill the Venezuelan supporters of a Maoist takeover, so that they could install American lackeys. The mission went sour and the Americans resembled cats covering up shit on a tin roof.

The condition of our release by the locals was that I go on the internet and denounce the American government. I was to confirm the reports that the "Americans used DEA drug operations to destroy the peace and quiet of established Venezuelan democracy."

I'm neither a patriot nor a fool. I denounced my government for interfering in the sovereign affairs of the Venezuelan government, and I meant it. I was fed up with the American government intruding into everybody's business.

The warning we were sending to the world was…

"The American government believes that they should determine how all other people live. Don't expect Americans to sit quietly while others try to destroy their worldwide influence."

I never could abide the arrogance of people or governments. My denunciation probably eliminated the chance for either my college or me to obtain future grants. Putting it simply, we would be on everybody's shit list.

Things change, the Venezuelan officials were pleased. I must have sounded convincing because we were moved back to our hotel immediately and treated with respect and kindness.

We were in good spirits when we arrived at the hotel, back from the barracks. The proprietor brought us roasted pig and bottled beer, delicious fare in any situation. We were relieved not to have to spend the next two weeks in a boring encampment, and we celebrated our release from two days of imprisonment.

* * * * *

The grant budget specified support for a second visit to the Waranii, so I was reluctant to go back directly to Caracas. No auditors would ever learn that we spent our visit in Puerto Ayacuucho instead of in the miserable indigenous huts of the Waranii.

We settled into a two-week visit to the jungle, softened by the luxuries of our comfortable hotel. As usual, I made the best of my circumstances. We could have worked on the dictionary but there was no hurry. We could do our work in the big city when we got back there.

Our hotel provided us the delights of seven-course meals served by indigenous lassies. I found myself fascinated by the chance to see what was trying to peek out of their skimpy blouses. I kept on dropping forks at my feet for the girls to retrieve. I hope I wasn't annoying the help too much with accidents that required the assistance of only the most exciting waitresses. I thought that never again would I be able to thaw frozen dinners and then eat them by myself.

We returned to Caracas after our two-week respite. When we departed for Caracas, we were escorted by an honor guard and the Governor of the Province. The trip went well and we were ready to settle down to do some work in Caracas.

Of course we celebrated our return on the night of our arrival. Nobody was expected, or able to go to work the next day. We finally got around to the dreaded day when we had to do what was expected of us. Wazu came over to my hotel and we got started.

My team and I contributed suggestions as to which 100 words should be selected for the final list. To qualify for our list, a word should refer to a palpable object or be very important in the Waranii life. Jungle plants and animals were among those first suggested. Personal things were introduced next; food materials and utensils followed. Within an hour we had filled the 100 spaces with items that I thought were most important to the Waranii. That was enough work for the day so we took a long break.

The following day we developed a second list with the English words, but written in Spanish. We used a computer dictionary to do much of that work and we were able to take a lunch break that lasted until the following day.

The next day I started writing-down Wazu's phonetic verbalizations for each of the words. We reassembled to do the hardest job, namely to make sure that the Waranii words really corresponded to the same things that were represented by the English and Spanish words. We depended upon Wazu entirely for that. We ran through the list as a check. I presented an object and Wazu would match the Waranii word to it.

The pairings were made easily if a word referred to a thing in a unique location. Pointing to a hand brought the corresponding Waranii phonetic sounds from Wazu.

The Waranii word for penis gave us a lot of trouble. The word in Waranii that Wazu selected and was pointing to might refer to the penis, the testicles or the scrotum. We sorted that out when I dropped my pants and actually indicated the part in question by holding it between my fingers.

That way we discovered that there were separate words for penises in both conditions, Wazu was frustrated in his attempts to get across to us that there was a different word for the penis when it was soft and when it was hard. A couple of tugs on mine and he moved his finger on the list from the one line to the other.

My product would be submitted to the Baptist leaders for approval. I would worry later about whether we should acknowledge the importance of the penis by citing several words for it in our list.

We had a similar problem identifying which part of the woman's anatomy was represented by a Waranii word. The confusion about the words for anus and vagina disappeared when Eva dropped her panties and pointed to them separately for us.

We had three columns of corresponding words in each language when we reached the end of our preliminary listing. Our work might satisfy a grant auditor, but probably would not fool a knowledgeable anthropologist. I had a surfeit of money in the grant so I decided to hire a consultant to suggest ways to help us hide our ignorance.

Professor Garcia was recommended to me by the head of the Anthropology Department of the University of Caracas. The chairman was an asshole like most department chairmen, so he recommended an assistant asshole to me. Dr. Cristo Garcia was a specialist in the *Qechua-speaking* civilizations of Peru. He was born and educated in Peru and knew absolutely nothing at all about the Venezuelan indigenous people.

Since he knew nothing about the Waranii, he diverted our task to adding a fourth column to our dictionary so that would show the corresponding words in the Yanomami language. His efforts were in vain because he was off the target of grant objectives. Still the squiggles enhanced the dog and pony show that I would present in the final report.

The professor and I smiled at each other a lot, especially as I showed him to the door. I was glad to have been able to help this innocuous old gentlemen put food on the table for his family.

* * * * *

Hurray! We were done gathering project data. I threw a big party in the hotel to celebrate. I asked Juan to bring along a whore from the Street of Prostitutes. He asked me if I wanted a special one for myself. I told him, "No thanks, I'll just watch you and Ramon enjoy yourselves. I get my greatest pleasure from observing others having fun."

We retired to my suite after enjoying dinner and imbibing a few rums. Juan proceeded to organize the exhibition, and soon he and Ramon were in bed with our very accommodating guest. I took my chair over to a corner and watched. The guys were pumping away and so was I. The girl was happy to get hard currency and the guys enjoyed their roles. I probably was happiest of all because I gratified my peculiar needs and at taxpayers' expense.

The last thing I did before saying goodbye to my team was to reward them. I issued grant checks to Juan, Eva, Ramon, and Wazu in the amount of $1,000,00 each.

The records showed the payments were for resettlement because we had disrupted their lives. All understood that the *mordida* was to keep their mouths shut. "There is nothing like money for fertilizing the field of loyalty."

* * * * *

I figured that the CIA or FBI would wait for my return to the States before arresting me. Arresting Americans in a foreign country means that you have to go through expedition procedures and an agreeable country always wants some tangible recompense.

A few days later saw me on my way back to the States, and all its dull routines. The four scotch and sodas I drank in the plane were supposed to give me the courage to face imminent arrest for sedition, once we were on American soil.

As I stood in the arrivals line to be processed, there was plenty of time to worry about being arrested by a goon squad. I broke into a sweat, but all for nothing. No suits pulled me out of line to clasp handcuffs on me.

It was all quite disconcerting-- nobody gave a shit about me. But the Feds didn't fool me. I figured that

they were waiting to pounce on me at their leisure. They
had all the resources and I had none.

BACK HOME

Ever since I denounced the DEA for complicity in promoting a Venezuelan coup I waited for the door of my house to come crashing down. Nobody molested me in Venezuela or back home. Nobody from the Embassy called on me, and there were no suspicious suits following me.

Two or three weeks passed by quietly. It was apparent that the CIA didn't want my denunciation of America to attract worldwide attention. I was feeling reassured that the Feds were not going to assassinate me or they would have done it already. It was easier for them to leave me alone than explain their involvement in black operations. If they arrested me the newspapers would spread my story.

Apprehending me would be of little value to the Americans. My public denouncement couldn't be undone. The only concern the vindictive Homeland Security might have was that I could turn active again and cause more trouble. I anticipated that they would set up surveillance of me.

I thought I spotted a suit outside my house, so I set up a test. I sneaked out of my house and walked over to a neighbor's house. I asked him to play along with me when I phoned him. Then I sneaked back to my house and telephoned him. I announced clearly, "I'll meet you at the Palapa Bar in 15 minutes and hung up.

I sat down and ordered a drink, but I had my eye on the door. Sure enough, the suit came in and sat between the exit and me. I finished my drink and I passed boldly in front of my tail, to go out the door. As I left, I looked straight at him. He thought that he was in dumb mode, but the look on his face betrayed smug satisfaction.

I had the last laugh because now I was sure that I was being tailed and that my house was bugged. This meant that I had to be particularly careful about indulging in my sexual diversions of peeping at women or following them. I had to retreat to my porno disks for pleasure. Nothing happened during the subsequent few weeks so I supposed that the Feds took me off the active list

* * * * *

Ever since my divorce my life was too chaotic to try to create a real home. The best I could do was assemble a changing group of beach weirdos to pass the time with.

I loved the beach life, but I was more relaxed with my small circle of Latino friends in Immokalee. They invited me to weddings, births and christenings. We celebrated name-days together, unless it interfered with my fun weekends in Miami Beach.

After the college granted me tenure, I took less interest in what was going on in Miami Beach. Some weekends I never left Immokalee-- I was happy there. I was grateful for the life I had as a bachelor. I knew I would never ever be able to be the husband and father required for a proper marital unit.

I was grateful that Maureen was rearing our daughter Annie in a proper Catholic environment. I wanted our Annie to have the moral training that I couldn't provide.

The truth is that I was also pleased not to have to restrict my Bohemian life and be bothered with the details of Annie's life. You could call me a selfish bastard, because that is what I was. I only cared about protecting my own frivolous life of pursuing improper gratifications. I was glad I didn't have to give it up to raise a child properly.

Annie came for weeklong visits while she was still small. I entertained her with the usual beach things, and I forced myself to live on an ice cream diet. When parent and child have so little in common, a week has too many days in it.

Annie wanted to make an independent visit to me as a gift for her 18th birthday. Maureen gave her the tickets and I was her host. The trip was to be a coming-of-age for her. It was hard for me to endorse her taking over the responsibility for her own behavior, when I couldn't control my own.

As I watched her deplane and walk toward me, I developed an empty feeling in the pit of my stomach. I felt like a lover meeting his returning lady friend. It flashed through my mind that we had nothing in common. Our painful interaction would follow the strict rules for avoiding incestuous temptations.

She trotted down the walkway toward me in her adult, high-heeled shoes. She swished her summer skirt as an expression of her freedom from her mother's direction. Who would control her now that she was here? I couldn't even control myself.

I panicked as the blood coursed through my body. I feared that I would faint. I was sure that she would notice my flushing and realize how uncomfortable I was about having a sexy daughter.

She threw her arms around my neck and gave me a big kiss. As her well-rounded beasts dragged across my chest, I realized that I had lost my little girl completely. No longer would I be able to throw her up in the air and catch her-- no more playing aeroplane, because her sexy breasts would be in the way. We couldn't appear together half-dressed because that's reserved for lovers or families. It was inevitable that she would become the newest target for my voyeurism.

Can you imagine how I felt? I was helpless to control my autonomous responses. From that time on, I watched her in all positions and circumstances-- all the while undressing her mentally! The falling feeling in the pit of the stomach was there continuously throughout her visit. I suffered a panic attack at the airport meeting, and I was always on the edge of having it again throughout her visit. It was like being nauseous but not being able to throw up.

The second night of her visit she went out with the condo manager's son. He was attractive and seemed to be a nice sort of a guy, but I had been "behind the door" enough times to know that sex is all that guys want. My chronic anxiety turned into a sickening nausea as I realized that I had fallen into the role of the jealous lover. "She's too good for him, she's mine and she belongs to me!"

I was alarmed because I had regressed to my old needy ways while I should be strong during her visit. I feared that a father's loving caress would turn into lascivious pawing. My God! I was afraid I might lose control completely and assault my lovely Annie.

I recalled how I used to masturbate so I wouldn't build up the physical pressure that might otherwise burst out in undesirable ways. I headed for the bathroom but masturbation only exacerbated the torment of our situation, and my anxiety increased. The week finally ended, and you will be relieved to learn that I sent Annie back to her mother unscarred by the monster inside me.

I realized that I had just experienced the longest week of my life as I said goodbye to my beloved daughter. She smiled sweetly at our parting and told me, "Thanks for the lovely visit." I knew she didn't mean it; she was being polite. She never came back to visit me again.

The same sort of problem plagued me again with my goddaughter in Immokalee. I became the Catholic godfather to the first child of a young teaching assistant.

I was honored to be her faithful Catholic guide in life. I wondered if I could set a proper example as a believer in God and in the Church. I was flattered to be offered this responsibility for another person's life. I meant it when I committed myself to being her guide and example. We celebrated her name day together every year.

Our relationship was fine until she started growing breasts. She no longer could sit on my lap and throw her arms around me in abandon without giving me an erection. I was afraid that I might lose control and commit improprieties so I spent less time at her house. Yes, it's ironic to have to admit it, "Sexual impulses could destroy my otherwise pleasant life!" I remembered Roy.

Few of my adventures ever produced long-term results-- I was content with the joys of the moment. There was one exception when I ended up with the semblance of a family. OK, so it wasn't a real family but it was about the best a voyeur like me could manage.

I was out peeping into the bedroom windows of the complex, where a very attractive young lady lived. As she was undressing for bed a youngster walked across the lawn to open her window. I slipped around the corner of the house but I kept on watching.

The young man opened her window stealthily and entered her bedroom. He reached out a hand and pressed a breast while the other was busy with his fly. She slipped down her gown and pressed herself against him. I pressed myself against the windowsill. Oh joy! They were giving me the show of my life. I loved seeing this youthful expression of love. She finished him off orally and he returned the favour. After that we all went about our business.

The next day I stopped the girl in front of her parent's house, on her way home from work. I hit her with, "I saw what you did last night!" Then I explained very pleasantly that I had a spare guest bedroom that the pair of them would be welcome to use anytime in the evenings. She spluttered and tried to smile. She said, "I'll tell my friend about your understanding offer."

They were shaken up because I caught them and made them face up to the consequences of their misbehavior. She begged, "Please don't tell my parents about it!" I explained, "You can be sure I won't if you make me a party to your action by using my bedroom."

They dropped by for a visit the next evening and I explained my situation,

"I'm a bachelor and sometimes I get sexual urges which I take care of without a partner. You could bring me a lot of pleasure if I knew that you were in the next room enjoying yourselves. All I would ask is that you let me watch you a little through the partially opened door. I promise not to ask you to do anything with me. I just want to share in your pleasures."

I enjoyed their company for the next few months. We said hello and good-bye but deliberately avoided building a friendly relationship. They were content to have a safe place to play and I never had it so good. The last time they said good-bye they told me that they would not be returning. They had rented a place of their own in the city.

* * * * *

Most of the time, in recent years, I stayed at home. I withdrew from the outside world and fabricated my fantasy life with the help of drugs. I never did use opiates. Only stupid losers mess around with morphine and heroin. I smoked pot because it was so available in the Everglades area. A lot of the residents of Immokalee were users and a surprising percentage of the population was connected with the growing, distribution, and sale of the stuff.

I loved to be able to lie back in disarray and puff on a joint without a care in the world. My whole body would tingle as it readied for the trip. Then without any exertion, I found myself in a vague, misty world, populated with entertaining thoughts and ideas. Life's pressures were lifted and I drifted into being a new person-- the kind I wanted to be. Guilt or worries evaporated and left me wholly unburdened. I could do anything I wanted to, and nothing could stop me.

Unfortunately, the effect of the drug would wear off and I would find myself back in my lonely world. Pot could be called the" Spectacles of the Voyeur" because it permits him to view the circumstances according to his own wishes.

Pot sure re-enhances a lot of things that you have been ignoring-- sex, appetite, the smell of the roses-- even the love of a kindly god. Marijuana encourages expansion of the soul. It's addictive only in the sense that it makes you feel so good that you don't want to give it up.

I could understand why psychologist Dr. Timothy Leary recommended that people, who were stalled in their lives, take LSD. It shakes up your brain so that, different connections in the mind can produce better functioning as you are forced to reconstruct yourself. Electroshock therapy seems to use a similar process-- kick the shit out of your old rusty neural connections and force you to assemble shinier, new ones.

The purpose for using these drugs is to provide a temporary distance from one's concrete world. They provide a respite, so that new perspectives about the self can develop. The extremity in treatment should be matched to the urgency of need. Pot and alcohol suffice for most of us.

Rigid lawmakers and strict parents are totally content to reject any mind-altering agent because it's sinful to feel so good. They follow the old maxim,

A Baptist is somebody, who is afraid that somebody, somewhere in the world is enjoying himself.

All religions are clear on prohibitions, but they whisper softly when it comes to pleasure and gratification. I always have admired the Muslim position on gratifying one's wishes, "If it is not explicitly prohibited in Islam then it is lawful." And again, "There is no hardship in religion."

* * * * *

My life was back to usual, when I encountered the most dangerous situation you could imagine. True, my Peeping Tom life was risky, but I never realized how dangerous it was before that night.

I occasionally took a night-time stroll in Immokalee although it was not my preferred playground. One day the sound of two arguing males attracted my attention. As I approached a side window of the house, the back door opened and a man ran out. Others continued yelling inside the house, and I thought I heard a shot.

I was afraid to leave what little cover was provided by the foundation planting around the house. While I stood there, I saw a man exit from the front door. The flash of metal in his hand suggested a gun. The street light illuminated his face as he moved away from the shadow of the house.

Shit! I just witnessed an execution, and I knew the shooter. Now I had knowledge of a crime and I would be at risk if the shooter knew I was there. As I scrunched down even lower, there was time for me to realize that I was at the crime scene and leaving forensic evidence of my own presence.

The shooter that I saw was a known hit man employed by the Cuban-Americans. He lived in my apartment complex, but we didn't know each other. I had been warned not to make contact with him unless I needed a job done.

He was not the kind of neighbor you gossip about casually, so I really didn't know much about him. In fact, I didn't know anything about the murder he committed right under my nose. I wasn't about to go around asking questions, but the next morning I did walk out to the cluster of news racks to get a paper.

The story only gave the basic facts which I already knew. The report indicated that some shots were fired inside one of the apartment complexes, but the police had failed to locate the shooter. No mention was made of finding a victim.

Everybody knew that the extensive Everglade Swamp had a roster of hidden mob victims. Maybe it held more graves than the record number of bodies amassed in the Hackensack Meadows that were tilled by the New York mob. These unofficial cemeteries were mob matters that outsiders wouldn't understand or care to know about.

The Swamp was wild and extensive. You could dispose of a dead animal or a dead person by loading the body in a boat and dumping it out in a clump of tangled mangrove roots.

The vegetation would conceal the corpse, but the alligators could find it with their sense of smell. Even the bones would have been chomped into bits and devoured after a few days. Examination of the alligator's feces would not yield anything recognizable as human. Without a corpse there would be no indictment for murder. This vast cemetery was nature's recycler of human body parts.

Nobody seemed to make much of a fuss about the crime and I certainly wasn't going to. That event completely cured me from taking nightly walks around the Immokalee apartments.

Encounters with other malefactors are not all that rare. If you were out spying you might interrupt a burglar. If he was scoring big, then he might misinterpret your presence as competition, and that could be dangerous. I had been lucky enough never to confront a thief.

A few strangers tromped my turf several times. Some may have been innocent passers-by, but some were inept voyeurs. Once I even encountered one of my former apprentices. We waved at each other genially. Then I made him pay the penalty by finishing off his nocturnal escapade right there on the ground, while I watched.

He wasn't sharp enough to turn the tables on me and challenge me to explain why I was skulking around the area. Perhaps his exhibitionist impulses won out because he was able to show off his male adequacy to his instructor. In any case, each of us went home with a warm glow.

One night I was coming home about bedtime after parking the car. I walked up to my house and found a young man peeping in one of my windows. I sneaked up on him and brought him down with a hammerlock. He whimpered a bit but I pulled out his wallet from his back pocket and ordered him to stop struggling.

He was subdued enough that I could march him into my house. He pleaded, "Please don't hurt me. I wasn't going to steal anything." So I asked him what he really was doing. He hesitated and finally said, "I just like to look in people's windows and watch them undress."

My reply was. "Great! You're in luck because I like to look at people when they're half-dressed too." I told him to take off his trousers, which he did. He went ahead and removed his undershorts too. He was too frightened to get into the spirit of our encounter, so his limp darling just hung there looking silly. I tossed him a towel and told him, "Go ahead and do what you planned to do while looking in somebody's window." He complied and entertained me.

I told him, "Get out of here and never come back to my territory again." He understood the part about not coming back, because I never encountered him again. He didn't realize what I meant about "my territory" because he didn't realize that I was a vulture, like him.

I generally discourage friendly neighbors because it introduces additional risk into my sexual activities. One neighbor in Miami Beach was persistent. I invited him to join me in a beer at poolside the second time he came over,"to borrow a cup of sugar."

I was attracted to this young fellow from the start. He reminded me of myself at his age. After Roy died, I never desired a serious relationship with another guy. I didn't want anybody close enough to me to interfere with my beach-based pleasures.

During our second visit, I brought out a six-pack to prolong his visit. I decided to bring him into my games without disclosing the full extent of my activities. I told him that I had to confess something to him. He was intrigued so I continued,

I shocked him with my statement, "I've been sneaking up to your bedroom window over the past year so that I could watch you having sex with your girlfriends." His response was, "You're kidding, right?" When I assured him that it was true, a big smile came across his face as he addressed me jokingly, "You old bastard!"

He thought a little while as he finished off his open beer and then he smiled again and asked, "Was it fun? Did it get you off?" I smiled back at him and assured him that it did. From that time on I knew that we were collaborators, but he didn't. He failed to see the full picture, so he apologized and said, "I'll see that the window shades are properly closed in the future."

I stopped him dead, "Why would you want to spoil all our kinky fun? You keep your blinds cracked and I'll do the same for you." He was getting hooked,"We could leave the front porch light on to signal each other when the show was about to start!" From then on I enjoyed one of the most ideal set-ups of my life.

My friend really got into the spirit of mutual assistance. He started going out evenings to the nightspots in South Beach in order to bring home trophies worthy of me. In turn, I found my own sex life enhanced by knowing that he was outside my window enjoying himself while watching me perform.

My colleague lost his job two years later and he went back to Ohio. I was as destitute as if I had lost a lover. I really had lost many lovers over the years, although most of them had never even met me.

After pining awhile, I tried to set up the same kind of arrangement with the neighbor behind me. His being married complicated things. The jealousy and protectiveness that he developed are admirable traits in a proper home setting. Unfortunately, they screwed us up right from the start. Still, it was fun trying to work things out and I did get some action.

* * * * *

About that time I had a scrape with the law. A party of students from Miami University wanted to liven up their lives, so they invited me to witness their sexual games. Somebody betrayed us, and the police took all of us into custody. The whole situation was bad because one of the participants was a girl under 16-years-of-age. It was assumed that I was the organizer of the sex party since I was the oldest man captured in their net.

The booking sergeant questioned everybody superficially. He concluded that there was no evidence to show that I was anything more than a friend, who had dropped by while the games were in play. Forensic examination failed to find any sign of my semen.

The next day's questioning affirmed the admission statements, that I was not guilty of criminal behavior. After checking some character references they released me. The police records for that incident only showed that I was interviewed as a possible witness to a crime.

* * * * *

Bunny and I had enjoyed happy lives together, but both of us were falling into the old married syndrome. Our sexual contacts arose more out of habit than because of desire. We had drifted apart and Bunny couldn't live with that.

She started looking for attention from other men and lessened her dependence upon me. She told me that she had fallen in love with one of her admirers and he asked

238

her to marry him. I gave her my blessing and we had the wedding at my beach house. I acted like a proper gentleman except when I exposed my real self and pissed in his champagne. She followed him back to New York and the last I heard was that they were very happy together.

In my old age I was getting desperate to arrange sexy experiences and I was becoming careless. The law reached out and caught me inside a Miami Beach apartment complex. The kindly old judge saw that my Dade County record was relatively clean and he felt that I deserved a short probationary sentence at most.

My defence consisted of the old stand-by:

"I was just cutting across the grounds as a short-cut on the way home. I drank two beers earlier and I couldn't wait to reach my apartment to relieve myself. The security guard must have apprehended me because he thought I was a thief."

The guard acknowledged that he had not actually seen me peeping in a window or with disarrayed clothing. All charges were dismissed and nothing was entered in my record.

I was back to the hit-or-miss vagabond Peeping Tom life when my luck changed for the better. Aimee, one of my party friends, lost her job as a pole dancer. I had known her for a couple of years and she had come to understood me.

Aimee asked to stay at my house on the Beach until she could get her life straightened out. I thought it might hamper my style a bit but it could introduce an interesting variation in my life, too. She assured me that she would recompense me for "looking after her." (Joke intended)

I knew that she was very liberal about sexual matters, but had hang-ups about intercourse with guys. Aimee was an inveterate exhibitionist and carried it over into her daily living. She suggested that she become my live peek-a-boo dummy and she would wear as few clothes as possible around the house. She promised always to leave the doors to the bedroom and bathroom open so that I could watch her anytime I wanted.

What more could a voyeur ask for? I was about to shout a jubilant "Yes!" when she sweetened the pot. She told me that she would give me a hand job anytime her antics excited me so much that I needed relief.

After two months of bringing me blissful joy, she found a rich widow with promises and a lot of money-- so she went off with her. I really loved Aimee-- I went into the dumps for six months after she left.

These encounters reminded me of the old saying, "SHIPS that pass in the night." In my version it read "SHITS that pass in the night."

* * * * *

As time went by and I grew older, it became harder to find accessible young people to serve as targets. Other old men like me would sit and look at the family picture album or panoramas of disk photos. I had been remiss in not capturing enough video images of my targets to support me in old age.

I found that now I had to go into the sleazy part of Miami to visit a house of pleasure that sold an assortment of pornographic videos. My life was becoming pathetic-- I would rush home so I could open the plain brown paper wrapper and romp a bit with my new digital friends.

* * * * *

You may well ask me, "What would you do differently if you could live your life over again?" I would have to say, "Not much! The only thing I regret is not making my avocation into a vocation."

One of my students became rich through catering to the needs of voyeurs. He was a pioneer in the expanding field of digital entertainment. He is now the Hugh Hetner of the "Housewife of the Day" fame. His company offers on-line subscriptions to enable you to watch a semi-nude chick go through all her daily routines throughout her house-- bathroom and bedroom included. Hundreds of thousands of horney men pay $100.00 per month just to be her virtual mate.

But I can't complain. My resources have been sufficient to live the good life and I have great memories. Once in a while I jog those memories by turning on my computer and spying on the "Housewife of the Day."

EPILOGUE

Narrated by Wilson H. Guertin, PhD

2015

MIAMI BEACH

Abraham didn't age well with the passing years. He retired from teaching at Immokalee Tech when he was 65. He realized during the first year that he should have waited longer to retire. He was lonesome and he missed being surrounded by the bodies of tantalizing youth. Although his sexual potency was diminished, his urges still tormented him.

Perhaps the growing impotence of old age was what made him so desperate. He no longer was a voyeur; he had become a dirty old man. He had to leave the midnight spying to youths, who could outrun pursuers. In short, he became incompetent and careless. .

His career of dodging the law could end only one way-- with detention. He was too old to have to do time, but none-the-less he had to serve a two-year term for public indecency. He was 68-years-old by the time he finished his incarceration. By the time the probation officer signed the completion form he was 73.

The incarceration late in his career disheartened him. He no longer had confidence and he felt useless. He seldom had guests anymore, so he closed off two of his four bedrooms in the Miami Beach house. He didn't go to Immokalee very often so he sold his small house there. He stored the accumulations of junk from a worthless life in those two rooms that had once been part of his love palace. He was becoming a hermit as he wound down his life.

As time passed, our voyeur, like other *rues*, lost his animation. His obsessive pursuits were fewer and less adventurous. The stalking animal became the reader of romance fiction. Instead of seeking the excitement provided by live prey, he settled for wrinkled pages of Playboy. He would caresses the pictures with trembling hands. Life was no longer exciting, nor did he want it to be. This was all that was left of the monster that used to terrorize the Miami area.

As more time passed, he looked at Playboy less frequently, but he still held firmly to the memories of what used to excite him. He would sit back and dream of how those hands that shook with tremors used to pound with passion.

* * * * *

Life was over, but he would not give up easily. As he closed his eyes, he clutched his magazine even closer. As he slipped away into the final dream, he envisioned himself as the dashing youth he used to be. He exhaled his last breath and with it went all trace of what used to be his irresistible impulses-- he was at peace.

May God have mercy on Abraham Murray, beloved son, father, professor; and detested voyeur!
Sic transit Gloria mundi. So goes the glory of the world.

The End

HAPPY VOYEUR

"There is no difficulty in being good. Every man and woman of mankind is as evil as he or she is capable of being and dares to be. It is the less capable, more timorous persons who are called good, and then only by default. The least capable, most fainthearted of all are called saints, and then usually first by themselves.

The Journeyer by **Gary Jennings**.

ABOUT THE AUTHOR

The author is Professor Emeritus in the Florida University System-- a Clinical Psychologist by training and a Cultural Anthropologist by interest. He writes under a facetious pseudonym because he tries to keep his personal life separate from his professional one. Finally, after twenty-five years retirement, he elected to share his varied experiences as background for his novels.

He has lived in Baghdad and in Cairo and has made more than 70 trips to Latin America, and 15 to Turkey. He is married to a wife from Baghdad, and he completed the pilgrimage to Mecca. Before coming to Florida, he worked as a profiler for a governmental agency for seven years.

Fifteen titles by Jonathan P. Slow are available from Kindle, Amazon Books, Barnes and Noble, and booksellers around the world. He declares that this will be his last novel, "It's time to *really* retire!" His wonderful children still hang out near the nest, and encourage him.

The author has written three novels to portray the working of the minds of psychosexual cases. He tries to help the reader make some sense out of deviant sexual feelings.

wilson@jonathanslow.com

MORE MUSINGS

JONATHAN
To me, Jonathan P. Slow is like a "best buddy."
We can go out on a Saturday night and have some
men fun, and leave the wife and children behind.
(Wives everywhere hate the both of us!)

HAVING A BABY
Giving birth to a baby takes a lot out of you.

PLEASURE
There's no Pleasure without Sin.

PSYCHOSEXUALITY
An understanding of psychosexual development is
the basis of all psychological theory

VOYEURS
All men are voyeurs.
It's just a question of how much interest in
watching secret naughtiness they will admit to.

PSYCHITHERAPY
Therapy can be successful only when the couch
becomes a classroom in which, to examine human
relationships.

PROTEST
There is no greater manifestation of protest than the shouts of those, who most want to share that sin.

GOD
You have to love God-- He has such a good sense of humor!

WINE
Good wine is better than sex, but that's just a 95-year-old-man's opinion.

LOYALTY
There is nothing like money to fertilize the field of loyalty.

BROWN FELLAS
Get used to them. By the end of this century little brown fellas will control the world.

MARXISM
A century after Marx's teachings, people still define ownership in terms of *possession*-- those feudal rights incorporated in Roman law. Marx forecast that ownership would be replaced by laws equitable to all humanity. We are still waiting!

A FRIEND
If a friend wants to make you rich, just route his messages to the delete box,

FOUNDATIONS
As the building is founded, so shall it lean.

MY BRAIN
I'm afraid my brain is getting old and ugly like the rest of my body.

LAUGHTER
There is nothing in the world as infectious as an infant's laughter.

ULCERS
People, who take themselves seriously, deserve to have ulcers
.

GRAPES
You too can become a wine aficionado if you can tolerate juice from rotten grapes,

NEW GENERATION
Kids these days pollute the world with their existence.

ADVICE
Become a psychologist if you want to understand people from the *inside out*.
Become a physician if you want to understand them from the *outside in.*

DEATH
Death is \no longer just an adversary.
He has become a sympathetic companion.

FOUNDATIONS
As the building is founded, so shall it lean.

LIFE
We live in a world of obscurity-- veiled dreams and infantile needs.

SURVIVAL
Is America fighting for survival or are we fighting for supremacy?

POPULARITY
Popular acclaim has become the product of those with digital knowedge and social skills.

LIFE
Life is sweet but short, so enjoy it!

GOD
God created me so that He could add my children as subjects to His theocracy, and so that I could make my undecipherable scribblings on the wall of civilization.

LIFE
If you don't appreciate W. C. Fields then you need a new perspective on life. Go smoke more weed!

.

AMERICANS
Good luck to you Americans. You seem to think that a few fashionably equipped commandos with

drones are going to disempower two billion little brown fellas and two billion little yellow guys.

LOYALTY
There is nothing like money for fertilizing the field of loyalty.

OLD AGE
I keep telling myself that it's better to stumble around like an old man, than have your relatives throw dirt in your face.

HAPPY VOYEUR